MARCO ⊕ POLO

FUER
TEVEN
TURA

ATLANTIC
OCEAN

Azores (Port.)

Madeira (Port.)

Canary Islands
(Spain)   **Fuerteventura**

Western
Sahara

www.marco-polo.com

FREE!

THE
TOURING APP

shows you the way ...
including routes and offline maps!

GET MORE OUT OF YOUR MARCO POLO GUIDE

IT'S AS SIMPLE AS THIS

1 go.marco-polo.com/fue

2 download and discover

GO!

WORKS OFFLINE!

SYMBOLS

 INSIDER TIP — Insider Tip

★ — Highlight

●●●● — Best of...

☼ — Scenic view

♨ — Responsible travel: fairtrade principles and the environment respected

(*) — Telephone numbers that are not toll-free

PRICE CATEGORIES HOTELS

Expensive	over 770 euros
Moderate	420–770 euros
Budget	under 420 euros

Minimum room price for one week including the lowest level of catering on offer (two persons sharing)

PRICE CATEGORIES RESTAURANTS

Expensive	over 13 euros
Moderate	9–13 euros
Budget	under 9 euros

The prices are for a main course without drinks

CONTENTS

MAPS IN THE GUIDEBOOK
(126 A1) Page numbers and coordinates refer to the road atlas
(0) Site/address located off the map
Coordinates are also given for places that are not marked on the road atlas.
Street map of Corralejo p. 36
Street map of Puerto del Rosario p. 51

(∅ A–B 2–3) refers to the removable pull-out map

INSIDE FRONT COVER:
The best Highlights

INSIDE BACK COVER:
General map of the Canary Islands

The best MARCO POLO Insider Tips

Our top 15 Insider Tips

INSIDER TIP **Big reputation**

Their reputation is as large as the Marabou stork after which it is named – the *Marabú* in Esquinzo, here you can dine inside or outdoors under the palm trees – and most ingredients are sourced locally from the island's farmers → **p. 79**

INSIDER TIP **Silk, felt, ceramics and... surfers?**

Wave riders and creative arts and crafts designers have together turned the strange and seemingly unremarkable place of *Lajares* into a mecca for art, handicrafts and surfing → **p. 44**

INSIDER TIP **Become an artist!**

Hundreds or maybe thousands have helped to build the pebble cairns in *Punta de Tostón*. There are still more than enough pebbles lying around. All you need is a steady hand, patience and caution: one wrong move and you will have to start all over again (photo above) → **p. 45**

INSIDER TIP **Pleasure to the ear**

Amateur musicians dominate the live music scene in Morro Jable/Jandía Playa and give it its laid-back style. Their genres range from Canarian folk music to African rhythms → **p. 86**

INSIDER TIP **Latin rhythms**

If you really feel like dancing, it is best to go to the island's capital, *Puerto del Rosario*, where things really get going on weekends late into the night → **p. 51**

INSIDER TIP **Culinary Canarian delights**

Even island inhabitants didn't realise just how appealing a restaurant in indigenous design could be – the *Casa Santa María* merits its new status as a culinary hotspot in Betancuria (photo right) → **p. 58**

INSIDER TIP **Parrot fun**

The *Oasis Park* at La Lajita offers lots of animal shows and entertainment and the parrot show is very funny → **p. 69**

INSIDER TIP Wild West

The west coast is wild and uninhabited and there is no better way to experience it than on horseback. The *stables at La Pared* will take you on an adventure ride → **p. 78**

INSIDER TIP Home of the divine

The delightful *DVN* (stands for "El Divino") lounge bar in Costa Calma with its relaxing ambience appeals to everyone and the best news: dancing is also allowed → **p. 75**

INSIDER TIP Island Art

The exhibition centre *Centro de Arte Canario* in La Oliva presents artworks by Canarian artists and sculptors → **p. 46**

INSIDER TIP Going down in style

Celebrate the island's sunset every night at the most popular after-surf party held at the *Sunset Lounge* in Corralejo → **p. 39**

INSIDER TIP A cycle up hill and down dale

Cycling on the island is a must and a good option for bicycle rentals and organised tours is *Easy Riders* in Corralejo → **p. 37**

INSIDER TIP Dive under water!

If you want to experience the variety of the underwater world – without getting wet – take a trip on one of the *dive or glass bottom boats* for a nautical excursion under the sea → **p. 108**

INSIDER TIP Sofa in a headwind

A unique way to experience the island is by trike, a three-wheeled motorbike. *Xtreme* in Jandía Playa makes it possible → **p. 84**

BEST OF...

● *Magnificent landscape*
How wonderful it is that the best of Fuerteventura is still free: the gorgeous nature parks. All are free of charge and freely accessible, among them the wonderful *shifting dunes El Jable* near Corralejo in the north of the island → p. 33

● *Visit the ancient Canarians*
Even the drive through a Malpaís – an uninhabitable lava field – is something special. Get a glimpse into the uncomplicated and simple lives of the island's original inhabitants when you visit the ruins of the partially restored lava huts in the *ancient Canarian settlement* → p. 56

● *Breathtaking view*
The best lookout point on the whole island is from *Mirador Morro Velosa*. From the slopes of the 645 m/2116 ft high Tegú Mountain you will have panoramic views over the island's northern valleys all the way to its volcanoes (photo) → p. 59

● *Open air art*
The *Parque Escultórico* (sculpture park) almost covers the whole of the island's capital Puerto del Rosario. The city exhibits the best works from the local sculpture competition held for the last ten years. A leaflet is available showcasing 16 of these artworks → p. 49

● *Cheese please!*
A friendly smile and tasty cheese can be had at the *Finca Pepe Goat Farm* close to Betancuria where you can watch the entire cheese making process for free – from the milking of their goats to the finished block of cheese! → p. 61

● *The wild west coast*
You can experience the spray of the surf at many places along the coast but in the little fishing village of *Puertito de los Molinos* there is also a beach and a duck pond giving it a feel of rural Fuerteventura on a small scale – a type of outdoor museum but without the entrance fee! → p. 106

 Dots in guidebook refer to "Best of..." tips

● *Wind, waves, World cup*

The island holiday experience does not get better than this: when the best windsurfers in the world visit the beautiful lagoon landscape of the Canary Islands they showcase their artistic skills and amaze the crowds → p. 111

● *More than just a hint of Rio*

The magnificent and impressive Puerto del Rosario *carnival* procession clearly shows what an influence South America has had on the culture of the Canary Islands → p. 110

● *Fish in lava*

The main reason why the island has become a fantastic diving destination is the underwater lava formations which are home to all kinds of colourful fish and sea creatures, for example at *Caleta de Fustes* → p. 63

● *Expert hikes*

The countryside may look desolate but it hides a wealth of interesting and wonderful things – large and small. You just have to know where to look which is why it is best to take a hike *guided by an expert* → p. 104

● *Living history*

The large and beautifully done outdoor museum *La Alcogida* recreates a typical village from Fuerteventura's past (photo). The village comes to life with, among other things, traditional crafts workshops which nowadays make their products for the visitors → p. 53, 108

● *Authentic flair*

Betancuria, a small atmospheric town in the interior of the island, has the most beautiful shops for authentic handicrafts and a rarely visited monastery ruin, providing insight into the way life once was on Fuerteventura → p. 58

● *Endless beaches*

Located above deserted beaches that seem to go on for ever, *Cofete* gives a hint of what it used to look like on the other side of the peninsula in the 1960s before the arrival of tourism and its large hotels. Of course, there is also the mysterious Villa Winter... → p. 89

ONLY ON

BEST OF...

● *Sight and sound*
Betancuria's *multimedia presentation* showcases the most beautiful aspects of the Canary Islands with pictures – and an accompanying soundtrack – that include shots of the fantastic display of flowers that appear out of nowhere after the winter rainfalls → p. 58

● *Shopping trip indoors*
The multi-storied shopping centre *Las Rotondas* in the capital Puerto del Rosario offers exactly that. When it gets too hot outside its air-conditioned interior is a welcome refuge from the scorching heat → p. 51

● *Art for a change*
Finished your shopping in Las Rotondas? Then have a look at what current contemporary art Puerto del Rosario has to offer at the *Centro de Arte Juan Ismaël* – where there is also a cafeteria → p. 49

● *Bowling, billiards and more*
The *Family Entertainment Center* at the Centro Comercial Atlántico in Caleta de Fustes offers a varied programme of entertainment for adults and children alike in an air-conditioned, indoor setting → p. 62

● *A poet's choice*
Still in Puerto del Rosario and this time it is a tour of the *Museo Unamuno*, the former hotel where the Spanish poet Miguel de Unamuno stayed – it is interesting enough to visit more than once – a fascinating journey into the past (photo) → p. 49

● *Dine with a view*
On the terrace of the *Mirador de Sotavento* you can dine outside, comfortably sheltered from the wind and enjoy a great view – a special combination because it is not often that you can do so → p. 78

HEAT

RELAX AND CHILL OUT
Take it easy and spoil yourself

● *Wellbeing – with chocolate and wine*
Every good hotel offers their own spa programme with treatments (algae baths, chocolate therapy, wine massages etc.) but the *Gran Hotel Atlantis Bahía Real* in Corralejo and the *Barceló Fuerteventura* with *Thalasso Spa* in Caleta de Fustes really do set the bar very high → **p. 40, p. 63**

● *Fancy a nibble?*
Foot pedicure at *Fish Spa* in Morro Jable: Dip your feet into the water and you'll feel an immediate tickling sensation when the fish start to nibble, you'll soon relax though and enjoy the treatment → **p. 84**

● *Take to the seas*
Sailing along on a *catamaran* from Corralejo or Morro Jable is a real joy – no engine noise and lots of space on deck to stretch out, relax and enjoy the sea and the sail (photo) → **p. 37, 85**

● *Cocktails on the roof terrace*
In a comfortable and relaxed setting at the *El Navegante* in Morro Jable where you can enjoy cool live music accompanied by a gentle summer breeze → **p. 86**

● *Chill out in the capital*
Sip some excellent wine, enjoy some delicious food and take in the fresh sea air and there is no better place in Puerto del Rosario for this than the *Terraza de Playa Chica* → **p. 50**

● *Holiday within a holiday*
Gran Tarajal itself is an open-air gallery, and the *beach promenade* has something timeless and magical about it which makes you forget everything → **p. 65**

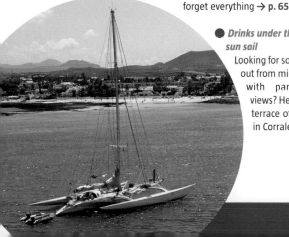

● *Drinks under the sun sail*
Looking for somewhere to chill out from midday to midnight with panoramic ocean views? Head to the rooftop terrace of the *Banana Bar* in Corralejo! → **p. 40**

INTRODUCTION

DISCOVER FUERTEVENTURA!

Surfing, diving, sunbathing, sailing, hiking or simply relaxing: These are just some of the favourite pastimes of guests to Fuerteventura. The island's charm may not be obvious at a first glance, but this is precisely what makes Fuerteventura so special. This Canary Island is an unassuming alternative to its neighbours and while offering many activities is really only famous for its kilometres of long-stretching beaches.

Dissidents of the Spanish regime were once banished to exile on the island, the most famous of which, poet Miguel de Unamuno, called the island "... a naked, bare, barren land of bones" – but also *"an oasis in the middle of civilisation's desert"* and "a country which hardens a tired soul". Once the most deprived among all the Canary Islands, this unpretentious island with its modest villages has definitely become an oasis for anyone looking to relax and rejuvenate their soul provided they are willing to try what the island so generously offers. All the sun worshippers and surfing enthusiasts who now flock to Fuerteventura also appreciate this about the island: its *primitive nature*, its wild landscape of sand, stone and shrubs and its remote location the middle of the ocean. It is an island that is an *austere symphony* of colours: white beaches, blue skies, azure waters, parchment grassy plains and gunmetal

For the recluse: Ermita de la Peña in the Barranco de las Peñitas

boulders. You will find no hint of the lush vegetation of La Palmas or the scenic diversity of Tenerife, nothing of the bustling city life of Gran Canaria. Fuerteventura remains one of the most sparsely populated of the Canary islands with a population density of only 61 inhabitants per square kilometre, and the capital, Puerto del Rosario, is a small town of only 36,000 residents.

Lush green oasis in the harsh wilderness

The island offers an ideal *escape* from the usual sensory overload. Here, the stress of sightseeing will not put a damper on your relaxation as there are neither ancient walls nor famous museums. But you should still take some time out to go on a trip or a guided hike to discover for yourself some of the island's hidden attractions – be it gorges, the lunar landscape of the lava fields or village churches – so that you can experience the spirit of the island. How about a siesta in a small fishing or mountain village? Because in the older villages one thing reigns supreme above all: peace. There you can sit underneath a canopy of leaves in front of the village church and enjoy the hibiscus blossoms, the sunlight as it dapples the pavement and feel as though all around you *time is standing still*. You can even lie on the wonderful shifting dunes of Corralejo and watch the sand as it is swirled around by the wind. Or watch as the setting sun washes the *landscape in light hues*: the hillside in wisps of rusty reds and pale greens and the gray-green lichen on the black lava rocks. The shadows move and almost nothing happens, but yet you get the feeling that you have experienced something great.

The happiest tourists on the island are probably those who love *water sports*. With their stable weather conditions and spots with all levels of difficulty, the beaches attract a colourful surfing crowd, and when competitions are announced they travel here from all over the world. Beginners can learn very quickly, as it seldom rains and there are no storms or sudden downpours. If the art of surfing doesn't appeal then one can always sail on a catamaran or try one's luck with some deep-sea fishing. The true quality of Fuerteventura is really experienced when one goes snorkelling or scuba diving; it has the most *fantastic underwater-world* and a plethora of dive sites along its coasts. Every diving school has

> **Surf Mecca in the middle of the Atlantic**

their own special site. Sometimes they can be quite bizarre – like the undersea solidified lava rivers – or just clear white sand or even some old shipwrecks, teeming with fish and other sea life.

The landscape does not vary a lot: there are some volcanic peaks and deep valleys, the occasional palm tree oasis, a handful of small picturesque mountain villages, even fewer sleepy fishing villages and here and there a modern wind turbine or a few old windmills. The coasts on the other hand are beautiful and varied. There are the endless stretches of *bright fine sandy beaches* of the Jandía peninsula, the pristine white dune beach at Corralejo, the dark almost black pebbles of the small coves of the fishing villages in the south of Maxorata while in the west *wild waves*

17th/18th century	**1730–36**	**1740**	**1837**	**1852**
Pirates repeatedly raid the coastal towns	After a volcanic eruption residents from Lanzarote flee to the neighbouring island of Fuerteventura	Citizens of Tuineje send English pirates fleeing (Tamacite)	The island's *Señorío* feudal system is abolished	The Canaries become a free trading zone; a boom ensues due to the export of dye, soda ash and lime

buffet cliffs with narrow crags and stretches with black or golden yellow sands. Even the surf is different: on one beach even ittle children can swim safely, on the next you have to fight strong winds and big waves, and on the third, the strong current can tear you away if you venture too far out into the surf.

Travellers who like educational holidays might not be very happy with Fuerteventura. For them the most interesting aspects would be the *rural lifestyle* of the earlier (and partly even the current) islanders and just how innovative they had to be with water catchment – all quite fascinating. Generally, it must have been very difficult just to survive on this fertile, yet inhospitable island. Immigrants from the south of Spain and France brought new agricultural and animal husbandry methods to Fuerteventura, donkeys and camels were used for livestock breeding and transporting water from wells. The *señores* had the say then, and over the centuries life was difficult for the indigenous islanders, the *Majoreros*. At that time there were only about 6,000 to 8,000 residents on the island. If the rain stayed away for long periods or if locusts invaded from the Sahara, famine was inevitable. Only the *señores* and the military were eligible for aid from the outside. The military was stationed in the only commando centre, the *Casa de los Coroneles* in La Oliva, which today is the most important historic secular building on the island.

Creative survival techniques

This impressive building – along with some old farmhouses and barns – have all been restored to their original form in recent years, and were either converted into museums, or into holiday homes. The island buzzword is *"rural tourism",* especially for those tourists who would rather be armed with their reading glasses and a good book, than with scuba gear. Aside from these small inns that are ideal for guests who do not mind the distance to the beach, tourists mostly stay in hotels and apartment complexes that seldom have less than 100 units and that are always situated close to the sea.

It is away from the beaches, in the interior, that you are more likely to experience the authentic *Spanish nature of the island*, hopefully during a *fiesta*. This is when bands play in the town square at night and people dance; there are stalls selling

1912
The islands are granted self-governance

1966/67
Tourism arrives

1986
Spain joins the EU; the Canary Islands obtain special status

1993
The Canaries are fully integrated into the EU

2008
Reaches the 100,000 citizens mark

2017
FFuerteventura receives the Spain Quality Tourism Award

snacks and young and old alike are out and about. On the main holy day a procession moves through the village, the dignitaries in front followed by the village folk in their full festive dress. These fiestas differ from the fiestas in the fishing villages insofar as there are no boat processions. But the party does not stop with fiestas and carnival. Nowadays the traditional dates are overshadowed by new tourist draw cards – the large international events which for many are reason alone to travel. This is especially true for the annual *Windsurfing World Championships* at the end of July or the beginning of August. The freestyle surfers in particular attract a lot of spectators with their acrobatic antics. In January, music enthusiasts flock to the Music Festival, and in early November during the International Kite Festival the heavens above the shifting sand dunes are filled with imaginative and colourful kites.

Fiesta de Santo Domingo

Fortunately in this respect some *variety* is offered. Guided bicycle tours and hikes with varying grades of difficulty are the most accessible to do. More exciting are the motorbike or quad bike tours and If you want to learn more about the island, you will find some excellent museums, art exhibitions and galleries. At the very least you should take a daily walk on the beach, because there is no better way to restore your soul, spirit and body by striding out on the sand listening to the *music of the wind and the waves*. And when the last evening approaches, how to say goodbye? Another beach party? A paella with fresh seafood in the hotel restaurant? Drink sangria at the pool bar? Perhaps it would be a good idea to take one last drive to one of the sleepy fishing

Processions, surfers and kites

villages, where, on the beach terrace of a small *bar-restaurante* you can enjoy some delicious fresh fish, drink some chilled local wine, listen to the *sound of the breaking waves* and feel the trade winds tug at your hair...

WHAT'S HOT

1 Fresh from the fields

Regional products Fuerteventura is a self-sufficient island, known for its home-grown tomatoes or Aloe vera. Yet the island is also host to many original farmers' markets, for example in Puerto del Rosario, at the Oasis Park or in La Oliva which are used by local producers to exclusively sell their products grown on the island. The better restaurants also source their fresh vegetables from the island's farmers wherever possible. One farmer who has made a name for himself is a German: Björn Mühlen *(bjoernmuehlen.com)*. His farm is located in the valley of Tarajalejo.

Recycled Art   2

One man's rubbish is another man's treasure Surfers not only love clean water, they also want to keep the beaches clean too. It seemed like an obvious idea to creatively recycle the plastic waste washed up on the island's beaches. Julian Blasco showcases his artworks in the *Clean Ocean Project (www.cleanocean project.org)* store in Cotillo while Luis de Dios collaborates on *Project Vortex (www.projectvortex.org)*, a non-profit, global collective of artists and designers actively working with plastic waste. Luis was previously involved in creating *Skeleton Sea,* a group of artists whose work is posted at *www.skeletonsea.com/artgallery.* Recycled art is a trend which has expanded beyond the island's shores.

3   Gin is in

Learning on holiday You can either educate yourself beforehand or use your time on Fuerteventura wisely and learn more about gin. Locals are becoming increasingly interested in the types of gin available and bartenders like to show off their prep skills — one good reason to take a seat at the bar!

Romantically rural

Casas Rurales A number of small country hotels have joined forces with the 🌐 *Casas Rurales* programme offering rural cottages with an eco-tourism slant. Tinín Martínez and Zaragoza Estévez manage *Mahoh Villaverde (C/ Francisco Bordón Méndez 1 | Villaverde)*. Their guests sleep in rustic rooms in a farmhouse dating back to the 19th century. The *Casa Tamasite (C(Tamasite 9 | Tuineje)* has old wood beam ceilings and antiques. In the past animals were kept in the *Casa de la Burra (Puerto del Rosario) (photo)* which dates back to the 14th century. Today the *finca* makes use of modern technology, in the form of solar energy and water treatment plants without destroying the charm of this hotel. Some of the houses are so close to nature that they can literally offer "holidays on the farm".

Street music

From Bach to jazz More and more musicians from all different genres can be seen busking in the pedestrianised zones and along the promenades of the island's tourist resorts. Some are holidaymakers who share a passion for music and get together for a jamming session, while others have been invited to play at large outdoor concerts organised by the local community. And then there are the brass band processions with local pupils marching along which can get so loud that other street musicians are forced to take a break.

IN A NUTSHELL

A LAVA OUTCROP?

Volcanoes dominate the landscape of the oldest island in the Canary Islands, especially the distinct volcanic cones which overshadow the regions in the north and around Tuineje. But unlike its neighbour Lanzarote which is still volcanically active on its surface, the majority of Fuerteventura has been formed by eruptions in the seabed. The three enormous volcanoes, which once soared over the island, have gradually been eroded by wind and rain over millions of years. It is estimated that the largest of the three volcanoes once stood 3000 metres high. Despite this erosion, the island is still covered in lava particularly in the north where fire and lava spewed out of vents around 10,000 years ago. The south also

has grey-black lava fields which the locals call *malpaís,* or bad land, due to the infertile desert terrain where only the island's goats roam looking for grass to chew on.

P IRATES, THIEVES, ADVENTURERS

In bygone days, a sea voyage was always an adventure especially in the wide open seas without a coastline to follow. In this respect, the conquerors of the Canary Islands must have been a courageous group of sailors. Unfortunately the tale does not stop there: Jean de Béthencourt was a swindler and a cheat who had been forced to flee his home in Normandy. With his ferocious band of swashbuckling pirates, he captured the island

Some interesting facts about Fuerteventura: the people, the flora and fauna, nature conservation and energy production

in 1403 with the support of the Spanish king and the blessing of the Pope who saw the conquest as a religious crusade to convert the non-believers. Those indigenous Canary Islanders who escaped with their lives were then sold as slaves and forced to convert to Christianity: in other words, state piracy under the pretext of religion.

Over time, the island endured many pirate raids, especially from the British. They invaded coastal villages which is why the island's former capital, Betancuria, is cleverly hidden behind the mountains (which unfortunately did not always protect the town). Houses were built from locally sourced stone to make villages appear invisible – the buildings were only white washed after the invasions stopped. The last group of adventurers to discover the island were of a completely different nature: Brits in

The dusky grouper, a fearsome underwater creature

search of a new idyllic holiday destination arrived in the mid-1960s and heralded the era of mass tourism. They have changed the face of the island more than all the thieves and pirates put together and have made the island what it is today.

DUSKY GROUPERS AND BARBARY GROUND SQUIRRELS

Those who enjoy wildlife watching will appreciate the barren wilderness Fuerteventura has to offer. Hiking through the landscape you will often spot lizards before they dart into the rocks on approach. Families of Barbary ground squirrels (similar to chipmunks) also build their habitat between the rocks. This species of squirrel was first introduced to the island in 1972 when a miner brought back a pair from the Sahara which then escaped. The squirrels can often be seen in places where they are fed by tourists.

Birdlife on the island is very diverse and there are numerous birds of prey like ravens and white vultures and of course seabirds and seagulls. On the tranquil beaches the busy Sanderlings rush along the edge of the surf looking for food while the hoopoes make their nests in the valleys of the west and the rare Hubara Bustards live in the dunes of the north. When there is an increase in the rainfall, the partridges flourish. The rather nondescript wild canary can be found here in its natural habitat.

The sea around the Canary Islands is very rich in marine life and the coastal waters teem with several bass species, mackerel, plaice, eels, rays, dogfish, blue shark, sole, swordfish, tuna and squid. During spring the jellyfish arrive – especially in the waters on the west and the south – and a sting from one of their long tentacles can cause some unpleasant burning and in some cases even paralysis.

DESERT FLOWERS

Typical of the semi-desert vegetation of the island is its low scrubland of yellow *lactuca* and other wild flowers. Plants that have adapted to the drought are the rosette-like succulents, the spiky Euphorbia bush, as well as the agave plants which were brought in from Central America and used for the production of sisal. The prickly pear cactus was imported from America and this plant is the host to the cochineal beetle from which red dye is obtained. Since the development of chemical colours, the need for cochineals had declined dramatically. The only indigenous tree, the Canary palm, grows in the island's oases while tamarisks grow in those ravines that have water flowing throughout the year. In February, the yellow blossoms of the mimosa bushes announce the coming of spring.

PRECIOUS SEMI-DESERT

Fuerteventura has every reason to be proud: Unesco declared the whole of the island and the surrounding ocean a Biosphere Reserve. What makes this semi-desert land quite so special is not evident at first glance; Fuerteventura has fewer species of plants and animals than all the other Islands in the Canaries. However this wilderness is also what makes the island so special and fascinates biologists who study how plants have adapted to the arid conditions with only a light rainfall in winter. In contrast, the underwater world is rich in marine life and every diving centre on the island has photos to illustrate it. There is a lot to see even for those who are new to scuba-diving. Back on shore, the island's exceptional landscape is protected by numerous nature reserves. This conservation movement began in 1982 when the dunes of Corralejo were declared a nature reserve followed by the Jandía peninsula. The best way to explore the island's natural beauty is to join a guided hiking tour.

IN WINTER'S REALM

No other person on the Canary Islands – certainly not during the 20th century – has ever given rise to as many myths and legends as the former landlord of the Jandía peninsula and the owner of the mysterious Villa Winter, Gustav Winter. Born in 1893 in Germany (he died in 1971 in Las Palmas) he came to Gran Canaria in 1926 as an engineer to build a power plant. In 1937 he leased the entire Jandía peninsula and built a villa. Rumours suggest that the villa had something to do with the German Reich setting up a naval base and airport in the Canary Islands. This idea never came into being, mainly because General Franco ordered Spain's neutrality during World War II and by that time Winter was no longer in the Canaries. The real era of rumour and myths around Winter began after 1946, when he returned and the peninsula was transformed into an agricultural operation (especially tomato crops and livestock) and the inhabitants were apparently treated like serfs. Winter never actually lived in the remote villa near Cofete.

CONSTANT DRIPPING

There is a real water shortage on the island. It rains way too seldom, and when it does, eight tenths of the water run straight off into the sea. Even before the introduction of water pumping windmills (imported from the USA in the 19th century), when the water table was not that low it was necessary for the locals to be prudent with their precious water resources. Fields were terraced, water collection tanks were installed on the slopes and domestic cisterns built. The water collected in the cisterns still had to be processed so that it could be drinkable and the limestone filtration ponds that were built can still be seen in some of the island's museums. Groundwater was hauled (and still is) from brick wells (pozos), either by windmills or by animals turning the capstan wheel. This water is also stored in enclosed reservoirs but is mostly used for irrigation or as drinking water for livestock.

Today, because of tourism, the increased water need is met by the desalination of seawater. Not all homes on the island are connected to the mains and many still have their drinking water delivered by a tanker.

MAJOREROS, MAXORATA

The J and X in these two words sound identical and are the Spanish equivalent to the Scottish (or German) "ch" as in "loch". Why then you may ask do the islanders write Maxorata instead of Majorata? The simple answer is this is the way it has always been and this is the way it will always be! In geographical terms, Maxorata is used to describe the entire island except for Jandía, the peninsula in the bottom left of the island. And Majoreros are the native islanders. Up until the 19th century Jandía was an uninhabited region. The word "Fuerteventurean" does not exist. Today indigenous Majoreros are a minority on Fuerteventura. The growth of the island's tourism industry has seen Spaniards come over from the mainland to work here. To meet Majoreros, you have to travel further inland. Only those who owned land near the island's beaches have become rich from tourism. Most locals do not profit from the money spent by the two million guests who visit the island each year.

CELEBRITY STATUS

Who is the most famous Majorero? Unfortunately for the island's government, the names of famous people born on Fuerteventura do not ring a bell with many; for example the writer, painter and art critic Josefina Plà (1903–99) who anyway emigrated to Paraguay in 1926. Over the years however the island has provided a second home to many famous figures. The poet Miguel de Unamuno was exiled to the island under the Franco regime and today the island's largest statue is dedicated to him. The occasional movie star can also be spotted on Fuerteventura: the charred and eerie landscape has been an attraction for movie directors to shoot their films on the island. Sir Ridley Scott set his biblical movie *Exodus* there while Fuerteventura was also used as a backdrop by Sacha Baron Cohen for his movie *The Dictator,* as well as for the action movies *Fast & Furious 6* and *The Invader.* And Morro Jable's beach promenade is set to be named after the former German chancellor Willy Brandt, who rode a donkey here in 1972 and is reported to have said: "A political equilibrium is defined by not falling off."

SAFE HAVEN FOR SEA TURTLES

Cofete beach was a hive of activity when her Majesty Queen Sofia of Spain travelled there in person closely followed by an entourage of journalists, TV cameras and the island's VIPs – and all in aid of a group of baby turtles. These small creatures were to make amends for ecological damage that once caused their extinction at Cofete beach. Known among biologists as loggerhead sea turtles, these reptiles used to come here on land to bury their eggs in the warm sand and wait for them to hatch in the sun. To turn the beach into a breeding ground for these creatures again, the first turtle eggs were imported from the Cape Verde Islands, hatched on Fuerteventura and after weeks of feeding and care (to prevent the tiny turtles from being killed by predators), the turtles were released onto the beach under the auspices of Her Majesty the Queen. The same procedure is carried out every year but without a royal escort. Conservationists are now waiting for the first turtles to return to the Playa de Cofete for breeding. If all goes well, Fuerteventura will have another attraction to add to its status as a Biosphere Reserve.

lava fields. This overgrazing has prevented revegetation and the island's semi-desert landscape can be attributed to humans or, more precisely, goats.

Although the majority of goats stay in close proximity to the farms where they are fed and milked daily, others are left to roam the island for months at a time and are only rounded up once a year in the autumn *apañada*. The meat from these goats (an apology to any vegetar-

The island's goats appear content even without lush green meadows to chew on

GOATING AROUND

With probably the exception of insects, goats are the most common species of animal you'll see on Fuerteventura. There are over 100,000 of them on the island and, as you can imagine, they contribute significantly to the island's economy. Goat farming is a mainstay of the island's agriculture since the land is difficult to farm and profits are marginal. The goats roam freely on their own or in herds in search of grass, preferring the sparsely populated regions on the rocky

ians reading) tastes extremely succulent and is often barbecued. Dairy goats are however more important due to the milk they produce from which the delicious goat's cheese is made. Despite the establishment of modern dairies, cheese is still made according to traditional methods, about which you can learn more in the cheese museum in Antigua or if you visit one of the island's fincas. Goat's cheese is also the perfect souvenir to take the taste of Fuerteventura back home with you.

FOOD & DRINK

Even in the days when the island was known as the breadbasket of the Canaries, the people here were certainly not living in the land of milk and honey. Today, most of the arable land lies fallow. But vegetables grown on the island (not just tomatoes) are becoming fashionable again.

Thanks to the EU agricultural market, the selection of produce on offer is now greater than ever – and quite international. Those who love Spanish cuisine can indulge in all the popular favourites like *paella or the popular tapas*, tasty little appetisers like bean salad, sardines or marinated mussels that are served in small bowls at the bar counters in local pubs. In all the holiday resorts you will also find a range of tourist foods like pizza and pasta, bangers and mash or fish and chips and nowadays the main tourist areas even have Chinese and occasionally Greek, Mexican and Indian restaurants.

But the best thing you can do is to tuck into the local dishes as potatoes and tomatoes are certainly not all the island has to offer. The menus always have a wide selection of freshly caught fish and if you stick to the *local food*, you will not only get fresh ingredients but also excellent value for money. Canarian cuisine may be simple and unpretentious but it also has some hearty flavours, without being too foreign. There is however one prerequisite: you have to like garlic as it is used very liberally in most dishes.

Photo: Fish with *papas arrugadas*

Besides the treasure trove of fresh seafood, the island's simple cuisine also holds a few other tasty surprises

A typical – and delicious – combination is fresh **fish with wrinkly salted potatoes** *(papas arrugadas)* and *mojo* sauce which is often also served with a small salad of tomatoes and onions. The most popular fresh fish is the *vieja,* a species of the parrot fish. However *vieja* is often only available in the better fish restaurants at the harbours. Even better (and more scarce) is fresh dusky perch *(mero)*. Fresh tuna *(atún)* and squid *(calamares)* are usually always available. If you feel like ordering sole *(lenguado)*, salmon *(salmón)* or langoustine *(langostas)* you should bear in mind they are imported frozen products.

Papas arrugadas are normally served with fish but they also taste great on their own or with **mojo** sauce. The main ingredients for *mojo* sauce are garlic, red pepper, salt, vinegar and oil mixed with a variety of herbs. This makes up the red version *(mojo rojo)*; the spicy red version *(mojo picón)* is made with

LOCAL SPECIALITIES

cabra/cabrito – goat and kid goat meat. The latter is a seasonal dish, but goat's meat (photo right) is available all year round. Kid meat dishes must sometimes be ordered in advance.

cerveza – beer; the locally brewed beers like Tropical and Dorada are to be recommended.

gallo – this is a fish that you will not often see on the menu. Gallo is easy to fil-let and has very few (but large) bones. It is special because of its firm flaky tex-ture resembling chicken.

langostinos – large prawns that can only be eaten by getting your fingers dirty – usually served grilled and generally the most expensive dish on the menu.

papas arrugadas – the typical Canarian wrinkled potatoes are small unpeeled potatoes boiled in saltwater until the water has evaporated. They are normal-ly served with fish dishes, but often also as a starter. With the potatoes (that are eaten with their skins) comes a bowl of red *mojo* (photo left).

puchero canario – a hearty vegetable stew made with whatever garden pro-duce is in season or available at the su-permarket. Everything is put into one pot and the addition of pumpkins then gives it a smooth texture. *Pucheros* is stew with meat; the best version of this dish is served at family restaurants in the countryside.

ron miel – honey rum is a great after dinner drink: a glass with a measure of rum with some honey and topped off with a little whipped cream.

sancocho – fish dish with potatoes, sweet potatoes, onions and smoked goat's cheese.

sopa de pescado – fish soup that is made with as wide a variety of fish or seafood as possible – all depend-ing on the catch of the day – served as starter.

tapas – this is hardly a Canarian discovery but these little appetisers are truly Spanish. People usually or-der a selection, for example *albóndi-gas* (meat balls), *patatas bravas* (fried potato cubes), *pimientos de padrón* (peppers with coarse salt), *mejillones* (mussels), *pulpo* (squid) or *tortilla* (potato omelette). If you are dining alone, two portions of *tapas* should be more than enough.

red chillis while the green *mojo* sauce *(mojo verde)* has parsley and coriander instead and tastes great with more delicate fish.

Typical fish dishes are the *sancocho* (fish with potatoes and goat's cheese) and the *sopa de pescado* (fish soup). Meat dishes are limited to goat kid *(cabrito),* mutton *(carnero)* and rabbit *(conejo)* and during the hunting season wild rabbit *(conejo salvaje)* is also available.

Goat's cheese *(queso de cabras)* is an island delicacy often served as a starter and when it is added to tomatoes, salami or ham it makes a delicious light lunch. The island's goat's cheese has won many awards and while it is now seldom made by hand, the form and quality of the product is still very traditional and as delicious as ever. The cheese comes in different forms of ripeness, some stronger and more aromatic, but all firm enough to cut. The firmest and most matured are *curado*.

Unfortunately the most typical of the island's dishes can seldom be found in today's restaurants: **gofio**. Gofio is made from grain (often barley) which is roasted, ground and the resulting flour is then made into porridge. This has been an island staple dating right back to its indigenous inhabitants, a testimony to the poverty of the island farmers, who sometimes had to eat it (perhaps with some vegetables or goat's milk) for months on end.

Wine is mostly imported from Spain and almost always dry. Spanish brands also dominate the island's sparkling wine *(cava)* and brandy. Mineral water is always served in bottles, either *con gas* or *sin gas* – sparkling or still. An espresso or *café solo* is a good end to a great meal. You can also order a *café con leche* (with a lot of milk) or a *cortado* (with some milk).

The local handmade goat's cheese

The differences between **restaurants** are negligible. They are usually not very cheap and of middling quality and only the Italian and Asian restaurants and a few gourmet establishments offer vegetarian dishes. Most restaurants, even if only seldom frequented by tourists, have menus in English, even if the waiters don't speak the language. Although service is included in the price, you may still want to add five to ten percent to the bill if you've had attentive service.

In the Canaries, as everywhere in Spain, meals are enjoyed in the afternoons and in the evenings a little later than what you may be used to. Lunch *(almuerzo)* is served between 1pm and 3pm and dinner *(cena)* is served from 8pm to 10:30pm but in the large holiday resorts and hotels **mealtimes** are kept at times more suited to the foreign tourist.

SHOPPING

The Canaries are a free trading zone, but this is not something that will be felt on your pocket as the goods are not entirely duty free and transport and storage costs are high. So you may even pay more for certain items than you would back home. However, tobacco and alcohol are still very cheap. Before you buy any expensive products you should first compare the prices with those at home!

ALOE VERA/COSMETICS

There are large plantations of aloe, the lily of the desert, on the island. The plant has well known healing properties and there is a thriving industry of aloe vera products including ointments and natural cosmetics. The products are available all over the island but do remember that goods are perishable so don't stock up too much. Brand-name cosmetics is usually a little cheaper on the island than at home.

ARTS & CRAFTS

The variety of arts and crafts available on the island has grown significantly; besides the traditional selection of authentic products, local arts and crafts have become increasingly more creative and contemporary in design. One of the most popular souvenirs of the island is embroidery, and you can find out how it is done at the *Casa Santa María* in Betancuria. The table cloths and aprons are done in a unique style that is typical to the island. Palm-leaf weaved baskets and goods are made in the open-air museum *La Alcogida* in Tefía. Both addresses still sell traditional souvenirs. Lajares is the place to go if you are looking for more contemporary souvenirs with ceramics, gold jewellery, silk painting, felts, extremely stylish canvas handbags and more besides. You will also find exotic items of black lava jewellery at the weekly arts and crafts fairs held in Corralejo (Thursdays, Sundays), Lajares (Saturdays) and Cotillo (Friday evenings).

CLOTHING & SHOES

The island may not be overflowing with shops but it offers numerous casual holiday wear brands to choose from: While *Cabrito* and *Fuerte* sell clothing with goat prints, *Extreme Animals* use a goat's skeleton as their symbol; *Clean Ocean Project* is an ecological brand of clothing based on the island. There is also

Hand embroidered fabrics, palm-leaf basket work and natural aloe vera cosmetics are some of the local items that are affordable

a wide range of traditional and stylish Spanish shoes available which are cheaper to buy here than elsewhere.

LIQUOR

Brands from the Spanish mainland are well represented and Spanish brandy is good and affordable. Craft shops sometimes also sell the local cactus liqueur and *ron miel,* rum with honey.

LOCAL PRODUCE

Locally produced foodstuff will last until you return home and give you a tasty reminder of your holiday. Popular items are prickly pear jam and goat's cheese; the latter is sold in four stages of maturity, the firmest being *curado,* and red cheese rubbed with paprika. The small round *queso de cabra* cheese wheels also keep very well. Jars of tasty ready-made mojo sauce are available in many stores.

WEEKLY MARKETS

The mainly African markets that take it in turns in Morro Jable, Costa Calma, Caleta de Fustes and Corralejo are popular for sunglasses, bags, belts, T-shirts and the like, also for African carvings. Remember to haggle! But do avoid buying any fake brand names as you could get into trouble with the law when you get home.

A special memento of your holiday – mostly for the ladies – is to have your hair braided with colourful strands of pearls and beads.

The 🌑 farmers' market *La Biosfera* deserves special mention – it is full of local products sold directly by the supplier *(Sat 9am–2pm | upper floor of the bus station in Puerto del Rosario).* A similar 🌑 farmers' market takes place on Sundays 9am–2pm in the *Oasis Park* in La Lajita.

THE NORTH

Even after repeated visits, it will always be an unforgettable experience: that first glimpse of the shifting sand dunes of El Jable. Suddenly, a white dream world opens up before you with mountains and valleys of shifting sands, as far as the eye can see. This is certainly the most impressive landscape on the whole island.

The north also has some other unusual landscapes with row upon row of extinct volcanoes lining up in beautiful symmetry. Black lava rocks are strewn over desolate areas while further south the landscape is a study in russet and red; especially when the low sun catches it. Corralejo is the centre of tourism. Recently Cotillo has undergone a transformation in terms of tourism while retaining its traditional character in part. La Oliva is one of the five historical main towns; Puerto del Rosario, the island capital, is not very touristy and is also underrated as a tourist destination.

CORRALEJO

MAP ON P. 36

(127 E1) *(⬚ G2)* **The main tourist attraction in the north owes its appeal to the 7.7 miles² dune area of El Jable on its southern edge, which merges seamlessly into the beach.**

Despite being confusingly referred to as a village in holiday brochures, *Corralejo* has long since outgrown this status. Its vibrancy, diversity and international vibe are second to none on the island. The town

Fascinating contrasts north-west of the island capital Puerto del Rosario: bright white sands and barren black lava

consists of a densely populated core which is mostly inhabited by Spanish people and a wide belt of hotels and apartment complexes that expands to the south and the east. It has only been settled since the 19th century. In 1940, it was a small fishing village consisting of only twelve houses and when the first holiday apartments were built in 1967, the town had neither water nor electricity. The main road and the pedestrian zone, with its many shops and restaurants, form the urban centre and at night an exuberant atmosphere reigns. A promenade along the shore was a spontaneous rather than planned project where visitors can now eat and drink.

Apart from the Playas de Sotavento in the south, the ★ ● *El Jable shifting dunes* are the main highlight of the island. The white sand dunes are constantly shifted by the north-east trade winds and, with their green flora valleys and rare animals, they have formed their own precious ecosystem. The area was declared a pro-

At the beach in Corralejo

threaten the ecological equilibrium of the dunes and ultimately their existence – be torn down. However, there has been some small progress in the matter with the planned closing of the road through the dune area. Now the sand will once again be allowed to reclaim the road. Please be aware that driving on the dunes is strictly prohibited.

FOOD & DRINK

Nowhere else on the island will you find as many restaurants with sea views, as on the narrow pedestrian promenade with the rather grand name of Avenida Marítima. The *Marquesina (Moderate)* on the small pier has a solid reputation and their delicious seafood crêpes deserve a special mention. You can choose your own fish at the chilled counter, something that the other venues in the area also offer. There are generally only small differences in the quality and prices of the restaurants, and do not expect very personal service. Heading northwards (toward the harbour) you will find *El Sombrero (evenings only, closed Wed | Moderate)*, whose speciality is meat dishes. The interior, decorated in colourful cattle hides, is a landmark in itself. His neighbour, *El Anzuelo (tel. 9 28 53 66 26 | Moderate)*, is the finest and most acclaimed fish restaurant in the city with splendid cuisine, service and atmosphere (sea view through glass walls). The best tapas are served close by at *Tapas Oscar (closed Tue | C/ Iglesia s.n. | tel. 9 28 86 63 88 | Moderate)*. Ignore the less than elegant name and take a wide selection of the half tapas portions *(media ración)*. The best pizzeria in town can also be found here: *Big Wave (evenings only | C/ Jesús Machín Santana 8)*. Its speciality is the maxi pizza for two.

tected nature reserve in 1982, but by then a part of the northern edge had already been developed. The biggest sin was the construction of two large hotels, *Tres Islas* and *Oliva Beach,* on the most pristine part of the dunes. Although it was later proven that the buildings were constructed illegally on communal land, the owner (the Ríu hotel chain) in 2008 still managed to obtain licenses for the hotels to trade: ten years for *Oliva Beach* and thirty years for *Tres Islas.* Only then will the hotels – which

The bars and restaurants become quieter and cheaper the further you venture away from the promenade. The tapas bar *Casa Domingo (Plaza Patricio Calero 31 | tel. 6 74 11 01 80 | Budget)* offers a great compromise with a great value for money three-course daily menu and eye-catching exterior (fruit and greenery) and interior (maritime) design. It wouldn't be a real holiday unless you could have dinner with your feet in the sand. Leave the promenade towards the south: the versatile *Waikiki* is an institution, it also offers breakfast. Away from the beach is *Ambaradam (closed Sat afternoons | CC Cactus | at the beginning of Av. de las Grandes Playas)* where they have been serving the best coffee in town (from 8am) for years, as well as crêpes, sandwiches and various pastries. *Secreto del Sur (C/ Guirre | Oasis Tamarindo, Local 26)* supplies delicious ice-cream, also muesli, croissants, cakes and more.

EL ANDALUZ

Manolo and his Austrian wife Birgit are responsible for Corralejo's finest gourmet restaurant. It is tiny, so you have to make reservations in advance. *Evenings only | closed Sun | C/ La Ballena 5 | tel. 6 76 70 58 78 | Moderate*

LAND OF FREEDOM

This unique type of tapas bar serves slow food at an excellent value for money. It pairs five-course menus with wines to perfectly complement each course. There is always a vegetarian and vegan menu to choose from as well as gluten-free meals. *Evenings only, closed Tue | at the Hotel Lobos Bahia Club off the main road near C/ Gran Canaria | tel. 6 26 22 09 08 | www.landoffreedom.eu | Expensive*

MESÓN LAS TEJAS

The restaurant to visit if you're craving meat and fish! It fills up extremely quickly because of its great food. *Closed Wed |*

C/ Aristides Hernandez Morán 2 | near Waikiki | tel. 6 76 31 01 94 | Budget

SANUS

The new food movement is meat-free, healthy food, a trend sorely missed on the island until now. The restaurant offers delicious vegetarian, vegan and gluten-free meals with a friendly service and atmosphere. Flexitarians are also welcome with some excellently prepared fish and meat options on the menu. *Evenings only, closed Sun | C/ Anzuelo 4 | tel. 9 28 53 65 85 | www.sanusfuerteventura. com | Moderate*

SHOPPING

On the main road you will find almost everything, but the prices are quite high. *Dany Sport (Av. Nuestra Señora del Carmen 42)*, the largest sports shop in

---

MARCO POLO HIGHLIGHTS

★ **Shifting sand dunes of El Jable**
White sand as far as the eye can see – towering sand dunes that are constantly on the move → p. 33

★ **Night life with sea views**
Things heat up in Corralejo when the sun goes down → p. 39

★ **Isla de los Lobos**
The small black lava island off Corralejo is under nature conservation → p. 41

★ **Ecomuseo de la Alcogida**
An outdoor museum in Tefia to experience how the islanders once lived and worked → p. 53, 108

the area, sells hiking and camping equipment, swimming and sportswear and also roller skates.

INSIDER TIP *Blanc du Nil (Av. Nuestra Señora del Carmen 37 | on the lower Water Park roundabout)* sells clothes made exclusively from white Egyptian cotton in a variety of cuts and weaves. *Little Paradise (C/ Lepanto 5)* specialises in surfing equipment. On Tuesdays and Fridays there is a – mainly African – *flea market (9am–1pm | on the main road near the Acua Water Park)* selling belts, cheap watches, jewellery, wood carvings, t-shirts and towels. There are also people who braid hair, and don't forget to haggle! More tasteful: the *arts & crafts market* at the CC Campanario *(Thu and Sun 10am–2pm)*. The district *(local 33)* is also home to *Marumba*, a popular haunt for self-catering tourists and the town's best delicatessen. The store has far more to offer than the run-of-the-mill goat's cheese. Its exclusive wine assortment also includes bottles of rare Fuerteventura wine.

SPORTS & ACTIVITIES

In the town itself, there are a mass of booths and shops which run from the harbour along the main road to CC Campanario, offering virtually every activity you can do in Corralejo and around: from fishing trips, buggy, jeep or quad tours to surfing lessons. Most of them are agencies and the same tour from the same operator is priced the same wherever you choose to go. It may still be worth shopping around first though because not all agencies offer tours from the smaller operators which can sometimes work out cheaper.

ACUA WATER PARK

A fun day can be enjoyed by both old and young alike: choose to slowly drift along the *Río lento,* throw yourself down the Kamikaze slide or have a relaxing mas-

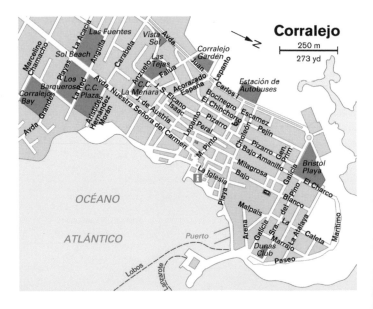

sage sitting under the waterfall in the wave pool. Youngsters particularly love this water park. *Mid-June–mid Sept daily 10am–6pm, closed mid-Nov–end March, otherwise Fri–Tue 10:30am–5:30pm | admission 25 euros, from 2pm 20 euros | www.acuawaterpark.com*

BICYCLES/MOTORCYCLES/QUADS

In the town centre, bikes can be hired from *Vulcano Biking (C/ Acorazado España 8 | tel. 9 28 53 57 06)* while the most extensive offers for mountain bikes, organised trips through the volcanic landscape and individually designed routes can be

Good spot for a rest on your bicycle trip: the small village beach at Corralejo

BOAT/FISHING TRIPS

Glide over the waves while fanned by a gentle sea breeze and warmed by the sun – nothing could be more relaxing than a ● catamaran sailing cruise. The price includes pick-up from your hotel, a walk around the island of Lobos, and stops for swimming, snorkelling and eating on board. The leading tour operator sailing from the harbour is *Fuertecharter (tel. 9 28 34 47 34 | www.fuertecharter.com, with an excellent video)*, but the other operators can also be recommended. The best boats for fishing trips are catamaran barracudas such as *Barracuda Perdomo (tel. 6 30 35 53 91 | www.barracudafuerteventura.com)*. Information on all the boat and sailing trips is available from the white booths along the pier.

found at INSIDER TIP *Easy Riders (C/ Las Dunas | local 2 | tel. 6 37 40 82 33 | www.easyriders-bikecenter.com)* slightly hidden in the east of the town. Electric self-balancing scooters are another fun alternative when the weather becomes too hot or windy. You ride them in standing to have the best view of the traffic. *Move Everywhere (C/ Hernán Cortez 18 | tel. 6 04 14 86 49)* offer a particularly cheap rental service. A motorised scooter is recommended if you plan to cover longer distances; hire them from : *LR Motorbike (Av. Nuestra Señora del Carmen 46 | tel. 6 84 06 83 62)*.

JETSKI

Ever wanted to race at high speeds over the waves? Then book a jet ski safari from

Swimming pool above the beach: RIU Hotel Tres Islas Pool

the harbour quay on one of the "water motorbikes". Booking: *tel. 6 66 14 15 66 | www.jetskifuerteventura.com*

MOTORISED OUTINGS

Buggy tours are a popular if not dusty way to explore the island. Guided tours on these two-seater, four-wheel vehicles are an exhilarating adventure; travelling virtually next to the ground, you head off road through the volcanic and dune landscape in the island's north. We recommend you try ⚘ eco buggies – all-electric, zero-noise and zero-emission speedsters which are permitted to drive

through the dunes. A fun experience is **INSIDER TIP** ▶ to combine your eco buggy tour with a camel ride *(booth in CC Campanario | tel. 6 47 28 83 39 | www. facebook.com/twizzylanz)*. A more sophisticated, if less eco-friendly and more expensive alternative are the silver, three-wheel *Canam-Spyder (tel. 6 19 07 22 48 | www.canamfuerteventura.com)*.

SEGWAYS

The alternative for all those who want to go faster than at walking pace: *2wheel-tours (CC Campanario | tel. 6 72 25 64 19 | www.2wheeltourz.com)*

BEACHES

Playa de Corralejo does not refer to the small town beach, but the dune beach 5 km/3 miles further to the south-east at *Tres Islas* and *Oliva Beach hotels*. About 1.5 km/1 mile south of the hotels, where the traffic does not yet pass close to the beach, is a nudist area. Take note of the signal flags: if it is red, swimming is not allowed due to strong currents and if it is yellow you should stay close to the shore.

SCUBA DIVING & SNORKELLING

Dive down and explore the underwater world of El Río. This low-bed strait between Corralejo and Lobos is sheltered from swelling, attracting a great variety of fish and making it ideal for snorkelling and scuba diving. Easy snorkelling safaris in the water off Lobos are available twice daily through *Get Wet (tel. 6 60 77 80 53, Udo)*, also for children from 5 years of age.

To dive down to deeper levels, scuba diving courses are offered at various points further along the coast. An ideal address for beginners is the resort's oldest diving centre, *Dive Center Corralejo (C/ Nuestra Señora del Pino 22 | tel. 9 28 53 59 06 |*

www.divecentercorralejo.com) with its own learner diving pool. Miguel's team chooses diving spots along the north and east coast or at Lobos depending on the direction of wind and strength of waves. The diving base *Punta Amanay (C/ El Pulpo 5 | tel. 9 28 53 53 57 | www.punta-amanay.com)* is a similar establishment. Both centres are located near each other close to the harbour.

WINDSURFING

Windsurfing, kite surfing, surfing or stand-up paddling – the choice is yours in Corralejo. The most popular water sports centre for all kinds of water activities is- *Flag Beach (tel. 9 28 86 63 89 | www.flag beach.com)* based at the dune beach in the north between the resort and the Tres Islas Hotel. *Billabong (C/ La Red 11 | tel. 9 28 86 62 07 | billabongsurfcamp.com).* is another alternative within the resort itself offering surfing and SUP. Both offer inexpensive accommodation for tourists. If you want the one-to-one learning experience, you can take lessons from a former surfing world champion: *Marina Taylor Surf School (C/ La Gomera 5/im Arena Beach | Tel. 6 86 77 66 62 | www.marinataylorsurfschool.com).*

ENTERTAINMENT

★ Nightlife with a sea view. Nowhere on the island offers a more vibrant and buzzing atmosphere after sunset than Corralejo. Evening entertainment consists of cocktails and live music in the town centre, along the promenade and in the bars on the pedestrianised zone (Calle Iglesia). Plaza Felix Estevez, otherwise known as "music square", is the main hub where musicians gather every evening to jam and everyone is invited to dance. The beats are louder at the bars and clubs clustered along the beach.

CHILL
The name says it all? But it doesn't reveal the bar's speciality: if you order a gin & tonic, you have eight brands of gin and six different recipes to choose from, making a sensational 48 types of gin & tonic to quench your thirst. *C/ Iglesia 16*

INSIDER TIP ▸ SUNSET LOUNGE
Come in the evening to enjoy the beach party vibes of this bar popular with, but not exclusively for, surfers. Crowds gather under the awning on the terrace with its windproof glass to quench their thirst with beer and cocktails. Louder sounds of hip-hop, house and funk are played at the weekend but caution the bar closes at 9pm (7pm in winter) to respect the local residents. The guests then move on along the beach to the resort's centre. *Av. Grandes Playas 75/eastern end of Galera Beach*

TEQUILA BEACH/BANANA BAR
A quiet evening stroll along the promenade on Saturdays is made difficult by the crowds of 20 to 40 year olds with cocktail glasses or beer bottles in their hands, all jostling between the resort's

LOW BUDGET

The water sports centre *Flag Beach* runs the 10-room hostel *Sol y Mar (C/ Bajo Blanco 7 | tel. 9 28 86 63 89)* right in the centre of Corralejo. The price of a bed in a four-bed room costs just 15 euros a night with breakfast included.

At the Italian self-serve restaurant *Da Uli (C/ Crucero Baleares)* in Corralejo, you can fill up for under 7 euros!

two hippest venues. The *Tequila Beach Bar* is also popular on other week nights with live bands playing on the bar's small stage – and a few light snacks for hungry guests. Next door *Banana* is a bar and disco (mainly funk and house on Thurs-Sat) with a spectacular ● rooftop terrace for those wanting to chill out – guests also come during the day to cool down on the sun-sheltered terrace and soak in the panoramic sea view. The Banana Facebook page keeps you informed of the bar's special events. *Av. Marítima, Ecke C/ Nasa*

WAIKIKI

An institution in Corralejo. Only here can you dream with sea views, your feet in the sand an a cool drink even at midnight. *C/ Aristides H. Morán*

WHERE TO STAY

ATLANTIC GARDEN

The 168 modern, spacious and very affordable apartments (each 41 m²) are situated next to the new shopping centre, *El Campanario,* east of the town. Three swimming pools and tennis facilities. *Av. Gran Canaria 4 | tel. 9 28 86 71 60 | www.atlanticgardenbeachmate.com | Budget*

BARCELÓ CORRALEJO BAY

Four star hotel for adults only; central, close to the beach and highly recommended. Some of the 231 rooms have sea views. Tennis courts and swimming pools (heated in winter). *Av. de las Grandes Playas 12 | tel. 9 28 53 60 50 | www.barcelo.com | Expensive*

LA CABAÑA

Five reasonably priced apartments near the harbour and the two best diving schools. Direct bookings only. *C/ Nuestra*

Señora del Pino 14 | tel. 9 28 53 50 39 | *Budget (without board)*

GRAN HOTEL ATLANTIS BAHÍA REAL

The island's leading luxury hotel. Three features stand out: its ● spa area (3,000 m²) with cosmetic and physiotherapeutic treatments; its four elegant restaurants serving gourmet cuisine (including one Japanese) and the hotel's high standard of service. Of the 242 rooms, 72 are suites as big as 1,722ft². You may never want to leave! *Eastern end of the Av. de las Grandes Playas | tel. 9 28 53 71 53 | www. atlantishotels.com | Expensive*

LAS MARISMAS

Las Marismas opened in 2003 with 232 two and three bedroom apartments and quickly gained popularity. It is situated in a quiet area (just east of Acua Park) and has both freshwater and saltwater pools, tennis and squash courts, mini golf and good child care facilities. *C/ Huriamen | tel. 9 28 53 72 28 | www.lasmarismas. info | Moderate*

SURFING COLORS APARTMENTS

The complex gets its name from the colourful frescoes and surfing waves painted on the walls of the 91 apartment rooms, all with a self-catering kitchenette. The complex is situated within the town which makes it an unusual yet practical base for your holiday. There are two small pools and you can also book a surfing course. *C/ Pejin 2 | tel. 6 70 77 71 89 | de.surfingcolors.com | Budget–Moderate*

INFORMATION

OFICINA DE TURISMO

At the small pier | tel. 9 28 86 62 35

WHERE TO GO

CUEVA DEL LLANO (127 D3) (*Ø G3*)

A large sign on the main road points to this 648 m/2125 ft long lava cave; follow the signs however and you could be in for a disappointment as the cave has been closed for some time. However you can

sion to this small island named after sea wolves, or monk seals. Because of its ecological diversity the site has been designated as a protected zone. This car-free island is virtually uninhabited and offers a walking trail around the island, a beach, a tiny village and most of all unspoilt wilderness. You can learn more about the

Untainted island: Isla de los Lobos off the coast of Corralejo

look into the cave and also visit the small museum. *Wed/Thu 10am–3pm, Sat 3pm–6pm | admission free | 11 km/7 miles on the FV101 towards Villaverde, then follow the signposts "Cueva del Llano" to the right*

ISLA DE LOS LOBOS ★
(127 E–F1) (*Ø H1–2*)

Ferry over to Isla de los Lobos to spend a few hours on a deserted wilderness. Those who spend their holiday in Corralejo should not miss out on an excur-

island's nature in the information centre *Centro de Visitantes* at the jetty. The island's landscape is distinctly different from the main island; here no goats or other animals nibble away at the vegetation, leaving this predominantly black lava rock greener and lusher than Fuerteventura. One advantage is the beach lies in close proximity to the quay (on the left) where visitors can relax and go scuba diving after visiting the island's lighthouse (8km there and back) or simply sunbathe in the bay. If you want to eat on the island, book a table in advance at Antonito in the village. You can also buy something to drink here or even better bring a large bottle of water and picnic with you from Corralejo. Remember to take your rubbish with you when you leave. And another thing, don't go looking for seals on the island. You won't find any. *Several daily crossings from 10am*

LANZAROTE (0) *(ญ 0)*

This island, which is well known for its natural wonders, can be seen from Corralejo. Boats travel between the islands several times daily, departing from the main pier. The crossing takes about 25 minutes with the normal ferry and about 12 minutes in the large catamaran. The travel agencies on the main road will have more information about guided day trips. *Detailed information can be found in the Marco Polo Travel Guide "Lanzarote".*

COTILLO

(126 B2) (ญ E3) **Too overcrowded in Corralejo? Then head to Cotillo, a former fishing village with an authentic feel that resembles how Corralejo was two or three decades ago. Although devoid of entertainment, the town is experiencing a growth in tourism.**

The main attractions are the beach and sea as well as beachside restaurants along the old port in the town centre. To protect the port, a defence tower, *Torre del Tostón*, was built in 1743 at the southern edge of the town, the only surviving historic building. At the same time a sister tower, Caleta de Fustes, was also built. However, by that time the era of the dreaded pirate attacks was almost over, so the old walls do not have any dramatic tales to tell. Today it houses temporary art exhibitions. The nearby lime kilns are testimony to El Cotillo's former economic importance.

If you arrive by car the country road leads you straight into the village. Turn left just before the end of the village and you will reach the tower, the lime kilns, the new harbour, various restaurants and a large beach. Turn right just before the end and you will come to the centre around the old harbour. If you would like to go to the small swimming bays and to Punta de Tostón, just follow the main road that bends sharply to the right twice.

FOOD & DRINK

Seafood and fish lovers are in their element in Cotillo. Particularly noteworthy

NORTH OR SOUTH?

"Don't you think the north is a lot nicer?" or "It's better here in the south, isn't it?" Those who have moved to the island to live and work are often so convinced that "their" part of the island is nicer, they never venture to other corners (with the exception of the airport and capital) and try and win guests (who have visited both) over to their side. To help you decide: the north has a more vibrant, urban and international feel. The south – including the Jandía peninsula – is more geared towards package holiday tourism and is better for bathing. You may be left wondering about the island's inland?

Rusty old cannons on the Torre del Tostón

is ▒ *El Mirador (closed Thu | C/ Muelle de los Pescadores 19 | tel. 9 28 53 88 38 | Moderate)* at the old harbour, where you can enjoy fresh fish at sunset on the roof terrace with panorama views. Even closer to the waves is *Vaca Azul (daily | northern side of the old harbour | tel. 9 28 53 86 85 | www.vacaazul.es | Moderate)*, which also has a terrace. The popular "blue cow" has really improved lately. The friendly café-bar ▒ *La Ballena (C/ Pinito del Oro 1)* to the far south of town serves cakes, cocktails and tasty, freshly prepared meals for everyone arriving after a day's surfing or wanting to enjoy the view of the fortress and ocean. The best time to come is at sunset. The INSIDER TIP bakery *El Goloso (C/ León y Castillo | at the northern edge of town)* is popular for good coffee and delicious cakes.

SPORTS & BEACHES

The beach south of Cotillo gets some large surf and attracts those who prefer waters that are a little more exciting, especially the bodyboarders and surfers. The *Star Surf School (Av. Los Lagos 42 | tel. 6 05 20 65 65 | info@starsurfschools. com)* on the way to the lagoon offers family discounts as well as stand-up paddling, yoga and aerobic courses. *Riders Surf 'n Bike (C/ 3 de abril 1979 33 | tel. 6 29 25 88 61 | www.riders-surfnbike. com)* along the main road organises kite surfing and bike rental. The conditions are not ideal for less confident swimmers and surfers and there are also a number of flat rocks in the water at places. The small bays to the north of the village, the *Playas de los Lagos*, are protected by reefs and the water here is always calm, making them safe even for children. In the suburb El Roque next to its windmill, the riding stables *Granja Tara (tel. Fanny 6 07 55 26 61 | also transfer from Corralejo)* offer riding lessons and hacks. Find an alternative means of transport at *Segway Tours (Av. los Lagos/Hotel Cotillo Beach | tel. 6 30 98 42 81 | www. segwaytours-fuerteventura.com)*.

WHERE TO STAY

COTILLO LAGOS

The name reveals where you will stay: right on the bays, the *Lagos de Cotillo* north

view of the ocean. *18 rooms | C/ San Pedro 2 | tel. 9 28 53 85 98 | Facebook: hotelsoulsurfer | Budget*

WHERE TO GO

INSIDER TIP **LAJARES** (126 C3) *(Ø F3)*
The island's most underrated resort also has an unusual history: originally a soulless farming community, the town has seen a transformation into a large surfer camp and Fuerteventura's mecca for arts and crafts. It all started with the embroidery school and the sale of embroidered items at *Artesanía Lajares.* Embroidery is

The beautifully restored Casa de los Coroneles in Oliva looks just like a fort

of the village. For those in need of peace and quiet there are 161 studios and apartments at affordable prices. *Tel. 9 28 17 53 88 | www.cotillolagos.com | Budget*

LAIF HOTEL

The former *Soul Surfer* hotel has changed its name and management. Guests rave about the hotel's central location and nicely furnished rooftop terrace with a

still practiced at La Pirata on the main road, albeit on a far smaller scale and has been the inspiration for many tourists visiting the island. All the arts and crafts on display are made in the town and you can meet in person the creators of these beautiful items. A walk around this creative community starts on the road to Corralejo on your left hand side: *Otro Mar* (decorative ceramics, *www.otromarc*

eramics. com), *Gusty Bags* (on your right; great canvas bags and cushions, *www. gusty.eu*), *Vaca loca* (on your left; fun felt plastics and jewellery made by Steffi), *Cabracadabra* (down on your right) with the silk painter *Lidia* (clothing, lamp fabrics, shoes) and the goldsmith *Bernhard Glauser* (www.bernhardglauser.com) and next door the fashion designer Ulrike with her store *Ulitxu* – and finally surfer art: *North Shore* sells surfboards, including hand-painted, exclusive designs by Sonni Hönscheid!

North Shore is the town's oldest surf shop run by the German-born family Hönscheid. Jürgen Hönscheid became Germany's first professional surfer at the beginning of the 1980s and his daughters followed in his footsteps. Sonni has also made a name for herself as an artist with her colourful surfboard designs (opposite the junction to Majanicho, *www. northshore-fuerteventura.com*). Surfers are attracted to both the north and west coasts which is why the strategically positioned Lajares, despite its inland location, has become a popular place for surfers. Several surfing schools offer courses and board hire including *Ocean Calling (tel. 6 92 16 27 65 | www.oceancalling.net)* and the *Magma Kitesurf School (9 28 86 82 88 | www.magma-kiteschool. com)*, both situated on the main road. Popular meeting points for surfers are *Mana Café* and *Canela Café,* the latter also serves as a restaurant offering more substantial meals. Live music is played at both venues usually on Wednesdays. There is a lack of hotels in the resort however the surfing centres have private apartments or alternatively *www.super fewo.com* offers other accommodation.

PUNTA DE TOSTÓN (126 B2) *(Ø E2)*
From Cotillo a cul-de-sac leads past the white sandy bathing bays of the *Playas de los Lagos* to the north-western cape 4 km/2.5 miles away, with lighthouses from three generations. The premises now house a *fishing museum (Tue–Sat 10am–6pm | admission 3 euros),* which is dedicated to the traditional fishing methods of the *Majoreros* and there is also a small cafeteria. In the western foothills you can partake in the creation of INSIDER TIP land art: over the years visitors have built rock cairns from lava rocks some of which are now daring balancing acts with astounding heights. There is a track that takes you on to Corralejo. During the summer months the area is full of Spanish campers.

LA OLIVA

(127 D4) *(Ø F4)* **Certainly not a stunningly beautiful location, but La Olivia is a popular destination during the day for tourists based in Corralejo – and for everyone else a stopover on a trip around the island.**

La Oliva, the main resort in the island's north, still offers a few ancient walls and is the main destination for contemporary art in the Canary Islands.

SIGHTSEEING

CASA DE LA CILLA
This historic building was once an old church tithe barn and now houses a museum dedicated to the crops and agricultural tools used by the island's farming industry. It has information about the agricultural equipment used and displays of old photos that provide some insights into the island's economy. *Tue 10am–3pm and 4pm–6pm, Fri 10am–3pm, Sat 10am–2pm | admission 1.50 euros | on the road towards Cotillo*

CASA DE LOS CORONELES

The two-storey residence with crenulated towers and 40 rooms is the most important secular building on the island. It was built in the 17th century as a manor. At the beginning of the 18th century, after the fall of the *señores*, the military government took occupation – hence its

underground exhibition halls and a large garden with numerous outdoor sculptures. Most of the works on display are by local contemporary artists. *Mon–Fri 10am–5pm, Sat 10am–2pm | admission 4 euros | on the southern outskirts opposite the Casa de los Coroneles*

Tindaya: a mountain that was regarded as holy by the island's original inhabitants

name which means "the colonels' house". In November 2006 the newly renovated building was reopened by King Juan Carlos. The interior has not been restored but part of the building is used for temporary art exhibitions. *Tue–Sun 10am–6pm | admission 3 euros | at the southern edge of town*

INSIDER TIP CENTRO DE ARTE CANARIO
The art centre was made possible by a private foundation and consists of an historic building, the *Casa Mané*, two

GLESIA DE NUESTRA SEÑORA DE LA CANDELARIA

The white triple naved church was built in 1711. It features a dark stone tower, a baroque altar of St Mary and a pulpit with effigies of the four evangelists. *No set opening times | village centre*

SHOPPING

MERCADO DE LAS TRADICIONES ✪

A small market selling fresh island products. It is held in a historical residential building, the *Casa del Coronel* (not to be confused with the large *Casa de los Coroneles!*). *Tue and Fri 10am–2pm | C/ Tercio Don Juan de Austria*

MUSEO LA FÁBRICA ALOE VERA

The focus here is on selling Aloe vera products, however you can also see how the plants are cut open and the liquid is extracted. They grow on the field next to the museum. *Daily 10am–6pm | FV-101/direction Corralejo on the left hand side*

INSIDER TIP VILLA VOLCANA
On the northern slope of the volcano Monte Arena ("sand mountain"), west of the suburb Villaverde, is a small house with a large garden and fantastic views. The four apartments (with terraces) have beautiful interiors and are ideal for holidaymakers seeking some peace and quiet. *Direct bookings only tel. 928 86 86 90 or 608 92 83 80 | han nelore@living-altlantis.de | Budget (without board)*

WHERE TO GO

TINDAYA
(126 C4) (ω E–F4)

After heading about 5 km/3 miles south-west on the main road from La Oliva you will come across *Montaña de Tindaya* on your right hand side. The almost 400 m/1,300 ft high volcano is made up of the marble-like volcanic rock (trachyte) and has a red colour due to iron oxide. The ancient residents considered the mountain sacred and left more than one hundred engravings of feet. Their meaning is still not quite clear today; some presume they are linked to the position of the sun in the winter or the summer solstice, the centre for a sun cult. Therefore, the mountain was declared a natural monument in 1994. Despite the fact that its historical importance was well known, in 1991 a mining company managed to obtain the rights to use it as a quarry. Although the work was later halted, the wound that has been ripped into the mountain is a testimony to political corruption which is quite indifferent to the protection of nature and history and far more concerned about the amount of profit to be made. Hiking up the mountain is only possible with a previously obained permit and with a guide. A little further along the road, on the slope of *Montaña Quemada* (126 B4–5) (ω B–C5) above a long wall you will see the monument to the poet, philosopher and Franco opponent, Miguel de Unamuno. He is the most famous Spanish author to write about Fuerteventura, although he did not come to the island of his own free will. His criticism of the Spanish government resulted in him being dismissed from his position at a university and sent into exile on Fuerteventura in 1924.

VALLEBRÓN/MIRADOR MONTAÑA DE LA MUDA
(126 C–D5) (ω F–G5)

East of Tindaya, a winding uphill road leads to a viewing point, the *Mirador Montaña de la Muda*. There is a parking area with a pathway that takes you to the actual viewing platform with an explanatory panel (text in Spanish and English). From here you can view a large part of the north-west of the island, especially the holy Montaña de Tindaya. If you time your arrival for the early morning, just before sunrise, you will see the intense red hues on the rocks.

Now the road heads eastward to the high valley *Vallebrón* with its little church village. Here, more than anywhere else on the island, some of the traditional farming methods have remained in use. This is in a large part due to the fact that the area receives a little more rain than elsewhere. Carob and fig trees grow between the fields and the entire valley is a nature reserve.

VILLAVERDE (127 D3–4) (*M G4*)

Although this settlement, which stretches out along the road to Corralejo, is seen by most as a traffic obstruction, insiders stop at *Casa Marcos (closed Sun evenings, Mon, Tue | on the FV-101 no. 35/car park above | tel. 9 28 86 82 85 | Moderate)* to eat at one of the best restaurants in the island's north. The special attraction is the food prepared by chef Marcos, the son of a goat farmer. Preparing authentic yet refined dishes, he only uses the freshest ingredients. His menu changes daily and the day's dishes are written on the chalkboard. The only dish which is always on the menu is *the* speciality: dry-cured, homemade goat's ham prepared according to an old recipe and served in extra thin slices.

PUERTO DEL ROSARIO

MAP ON P. 51

(131 E1) (*M G–H6*) **When you are on Fuerteventura: do take a trip to Spain! Because especially from the perspective of a resort area, the island's almost tourist-free capital is another world altogether.**

Puerto Rosario (the short form of the name) is not very old nor is it especially beautiful, yet the harbour town with 36,000 inhabitants is the liveliest place on the island.

From 1797 the town developed as the harbour for the nearby hamlet of Tetir. A fresh spring attracted goats and so the new settlement was called *Puerto de Cabras* (goat harbour). With the increase of maritime traffic to Gran Canaria, Tenerife and to the mainland, many Spaniards and Gran Canarians began to settle here. In 1835 the little town grew to 500 inhabitants and became a town in its own right independent of Tetir. Its growth and development was then further increased by English merchants who shipped soda, dye (from the cochineal beetle) and lime from here in the 19th century. For several years Great Britain even had a consulate here.

Puerto de Cabras overtook the older towns as the most important port and as the central entrance to the island, and by 1860 was considered Fuerteventura's capital. From 1900, more and more administrative buildings went up and the first hotel opened its doors. Gradually the "goat harbour" name seemed inappropriate and in 1956 the town was renamed Puerto del Rosario ("port of the rosary") in honour of the holy Virgin of the Rosary, the patron saint of the city.

From the 1980s onwards the overall appearance of the town has improved: historical buildings have been restored, parks and a promenade have been built and sculptures erected. Especially attractive is the town centre with the island's administrative seat *(Cabildo Insular)*, the church and the town hall. The improvements have also resulted in tourists from passing cruise ships visiting the town, much to the delight of its citizens and the town council. Puerto del Rosario also has the added attraction of a large number of cultural activities.

Here is one option for a local sightseeing tour: from the *Parque Municipal*, south of the bus station, where the two main roads cross, turn down the main road León y Castillo. The first building on your right hand side is the wrestling arena. Behind the arena is the rectory. Head to the parallel road along the front of the house. Further down from here you will pass the *Casa Museo Unamuno* and the church will be on your left. At the next corner you will see the *Cabildo Insular* (the island's administrative building) on your right and on the left the town hall. Further down you will reach the harbour and its promenade. From here, go back up the

de Unamuno (1864–1936) lived for four months during his exile in 1924. Also staying with him was the journalist Rodrigo Soriano. Visitors can take a trip into the past and view his writing desk, his bed and even his chamber pot and the kitchen have been kept exactly as they were during his day. *Mon–Fri 9am–2pm | admission free | next to the church*

CENTRO DE ARTE JUAN ISMAËL ●
The three-storey building, with its yellow gabled facade, houses atmospheric ex-

The poet's desk in the Casa Museo Unamuno

León y Castillo again and turn left at the town hall to reach the sizeable commercial centre which is also a pedestrian zone.

SIGHTSEEING

CASA MUSEO UNAMUNO ●
The museum is in the rooms of the former hotel *Fuerteventura* where the Spanish writer and philosopher Miguel

hibitions and event rooms as well as artists' studios. On display are contemporary artworks by Canary Island artists. *Tue–Sat 10am–1pm and 5pm–9pm | C/ Almirante Lallermand 30*

INSIDER TIP ▶ PARQUE ESCULTÓRICO ●
Some of the island's other open spaces have in recent years also been embellished with sculptures and statues, but

nowhere else are they as many or as interesting than in the island's capital: more than 100. Many have been fitted with explanatory plaques. The background: A sculptor symposium had been held here for ten years since 2001, and the best works remained in the city. Most of them adorn the promenade, but the *Parque Escultórico* (sculpture park) has no fixed boundaries and spreads out all over the town. A free route map is distributed by the tourist information centre and guides you through 16 of the town centre's art works. *www.turismo-puertodelrosario.org*

FOOD & DRINK

The same applies to all the venues in Puerto del Rosario: almost all of the staff only understand Spanish! If you would like something small to eat, you can try the cafés in the pedestrian precinct Avenida Primero de Mayo, among them the Italian ice-cream parlour *Kiss (corner Calle Maestro de Falla)* which also serves decent pizzas. A rest with sea views is possible at the terrace restaurant ☆ *Los Paragüitas (Plaza de España)*. Eating and drinking in an air-conditioned setting is possible on the upper floor of the shopping centre *Las Rotondas*.

EL PERENQUÉN ☆

The perfect stop for a light meal or snack during your tour of the island's capital! On its terrace with a view over the port, the friendly staff serves up filled bread rolls and baguettes, light warm meals, drinks, coffee and cakes. *Mon–Wed, Sat 8:30am–4pm, Thu/Fri 8:30am until after midnight | C/ García Escámez 5 | Budget*

INSIDER TIP LA TERRAZA DE PLAYA CHICA ● ☆

A table with a sea view is what you can expect at the terrace, in Puerto Rosario's chill out zone on the small beach. Trendy but substantial meals with decent portions. *Daily | Los Pozos | corner Guadiana | tel. 9 28 85 69 65 | terrazaplayachica. com | Moderate–Expensive*

Sports and fishing boats bobbing in the harbour at Puerto del Rosario

Puerto del Rosario

250 m
273 yd

Estación de Guaguas
Cuartel de Infantería
Casa de la Cultura
Biblioteca
Parque Municipal
Pabellón do Deportes
El Cabildo
Insular Rosario
Casa Museo Unamuno
Ayuntamiento
Plaza de España
El Encharco
OCEÁNO ATLÁNTICO
Puerto
Muelle
Universidad Popular
Las Palmas de Gr. C.

SHOPPING

LA BIOSFERA
The weekly market on the top floor of the bus station was established especially to sell the island's produce – everything is very fresh and organic. *Sat 9am–2pm | Estación de Guaguas*

LAS ROTONDAS ●
Between the first and the second roundabout southwards is the town's very conspicuous shopping centre – a destination in itself. Around 100 stores are spread over four floors and there is also a large parking garage. Instead of escalators, pram-friendly rolling ramps link the

floors. In addition to the usual (clothing, sporting goods) you will also find telephone shops, a bookstore and a Hiperdino supermarket.

ENTERTAINMENT

If you are feeling adventurous, you should leave your resort for one Saturday night and explore the local nightlife. Nowhere on the island will you find such attractive and authentic bars and as much INSIDER TIP Latin dance fun as here (e.g. in the *Mama Rumba*). Bars and clubs only open at about 11pm and smart casual clothing is preferred, that means no sandals, running shoes, baseball caps or t-shirts. In addition Puerto Rosario also offers some more sophisticated culture, like performances and art exhibitions in the *Casa de la Cultura (C/ Ramiro de Maeztu 2)*. Events are advertised on posters in Spanish around the town.

INSIDER TIP ▶ MAMA RUMBA

The most beautiful Latin American dance venue on the island has a wonderful relaxed atmosphere where every guest (regardless of age and ability) is made to feel welcome. One of the best choices for Saturday nights. *C/ San Roque 17 | close to Cabildo Insular*

MOAI

Puerto Rosario's new trendy bar for after-sunset hours. Professionally prepared drinks served in a relaxed atmosphere with Latino pop sounds. In short, the in-place for weekend nights in the island's capital. *Thu–Sat from 10pm | C/ León y Castillo 28*

WHERE TO STAY

Accommodation in Puerto del Rosario is very limited when it comes to tourists, because in the town itself there is no accommodation with terraces, entertainment and the usual tourist amenities. You only come here if you want to experience the weekend nightlife.

LA TIERRA

Fed up of R&B and hip-hop? Then head to the town's most popular music club which offers a platform for all budding musicians. Located amongst the pubs along the harbour, this crowd-puller is open not just at weekends. Wednesdays is jam session. *C/ Eustaquio Gopar s/n*

WHERE TO STAY

The choice of overnight accommodation in Puerto del Rosario is limited; admittedly there are no hotels with sun terraces, pools etc. in the town and the main reason for coming here is to enjoy the weekend nightlife.

JM PUERTO ROSARIO

Luxurious hotel in central location; almost all the 88 rooms offer a view of the harbour or sea. *Av. Marítima 9 | tel. 928 85 94 64 | www.jmhoteles.com | Moderate t*

FOR BOOKWORMS & FILM BUFFS

Pleasures of the Canary Islands: Wine, Food and Mystery – little book by husband and wife team Ann and Larry Walkers exploring the pleasures of the islands: food, wines, nature and the people. Chapter with traditional recipes.

Exodus – Fuerteventura as the background setting for Hollywood cinema!

In 2013, the island was used for the outdoor shooting of this film epic that brought the story of Moses to the big screen. Many of the island's inhabitants were employed as extras as well as hundreds of horses and camels. The director was Ridley Scott ("Alien", "Blade Runner"). *www.exodusgods andkings.com*

INFORMATION

PATRONATO DE TURISMO
Av. Marítima | at the large roundabout across C/ León y Castillo | tel. 9 28 53 08 44

WHERE TO GO

TEFÍA (130 C1) (𝓜 E6)

From Casillas del Ángel (towards La Oliva) it is not far to Tefía – a scattered, rural settlement surrounded by mountains. Some of the farmhouses have been restored and included in the ★ ● *Ecomuseo de la Alcogida*. The houses have been revived by traditionally working

landing strip crossed over the road which had to be closed every time an aeroplane took off or landed.

The church village of Tetir, at one point the parish church of Puerto del Rosario, is the focal point of this fertile valley. The terraced fields on the valley slopes – once used to grow cereals and prickly pears – are relics of an era when agriculture was still very important and provided the inhabitants with a degree of prosperity. Tetir's parish church (1745), the *Iglesia de Santo Domingo de Guzmán* with its baroque altar, bears witness to this prosperity. It is worth making a detour to the 511 m/ 1,680 ft high moun-

Ancient handicraft: basket weaver in the La Alcogida museum at Tefía

craftsmen and there are even animals kept here. Find out more in the chapter *"Travel with kids"* (see p. 108).

TETIR (126–127 C–D6) (𝓜 F5–6)

From Puerto del Rosario you drive on the old main road to Corralejo, past the island's old airport *Los Estancos*. The old

tain ☼ **INSIDER TIP** *Temejereque* (127 D5) (𝓜 F5) north of Tetir. From the broadcasting station on the summit you have excellent views of the island on a clear day. The access road turns off about 1.5 km/1 mile north-west of Tetir. Follow the signpost "Tamariche" and then go straight ahead.

THE CENTRE

This is where you will have your first encounter with Fuerteventura, because here – south of the capital Puerto del Rosario – you will land at the airport. The first impression is a sobering one: you will see little more than the gray-yellow monotony of the semi-industrial and commercial section of the town.

Tourists head straight out towards the north or south to the Jandía peninsula. But at some point most return to the centre region, because four of the island's five places of historic importance lie here: Antiqua, Betancuria, Pájara and Tuineje. The island's busiest tourist centre of Caleta de Fustes is close to the airport while the bays of the south coast are lined with picturesque fishing villages and friendly Gran Tarajal. The area is divided into a wide, trough-shaped extended valley with a mountainous area to the west, which rise up to 722 m/2,370 ft, and has deep valleys and beautiful palm oases. Some farming is still done here and the main produce are tomatoes and aloe vera.

ANTIGUA

(129 E3) *(ω E7–8)* **Arriving from the north, you are welcomed to La Antigua by the historical windmill housing the cheese museum.**

The town is surrounded by a wide valley that has been settled since the end of the 15th century when Andalusian and Norman settlers arrived and began to cultivate

Quiet fishing villages and palm oases, high mountains and deep valleys: this is the historic centre of the island

the red fertile valley soil. They founded La Antigua in the 18th century. Today La Antigua administers the surrounding community (with the same name) which includes the holiday resort of Caleta de Fustes.

SIGHTSEEING

IGLESIA DE NUESTRA SEÑORA

The white parish church – dedicated to the Virgin of Antigua – dominates the centre of the community. The large building has a single nave and bell tower and was completed in 1785. Don't miss the Mudéjar ceiling in the choir and the ochre-coloured classical altar. In the tastefully renovated square palm trees and plants offer shade. *Daily 9am–1pm*

MUSEO DEL QUESO MAJORERO

You love goat's cheese? Then let yourself be informed about the history of traditional goat cheese making at the cheese museum, which also informs visitors about the island's geological origins. Many regular visitors to Fuerteventura probably know the museum better as the old "Molino de Antigua" and in fact this small, beautiful-

the restaurant holds true to its name serving delicious Italian dishes such as goat's meat Bolognese. The owner Francesco is inspired by the island's traditional cuisine. Treat yourself to one of

Fishing boats in the tranquil Pozo Negro on the east coast

ly renovated mill is still one of the island's most important landmarks and can be visited by tourists. The spacious gardens surrounding the estate are also beautiful to see as well as the cactus garden at the back under palm groves. The museum also houses a cafeteria with a small shop selling different cheeses as well as other products. *Tue–Sat 10am–6pm | admission 2 euros | on the FV 20 north of the town*

their delicious desserts. *Daily | on the FV 416 diagonally opposite the church | tel. 9 28 87 87 56 | Budget–Moderate*

WHERE TO GO

POZO NEGRO AND THE ANCIENT SETTLEMENT RUINS AT ATALAYITA ●

How about a visit to the stone age? Turn off the FV 2 on to the cul-de-sac road to Pozo Negro, after about 3 km/1.8 miles you will see a road that turns right on to a new track. It runs diagonally across the black lava flow that follows the road to the coast and leads to the most important ruins of structures built by the island's

FOOD & DRINK

TODO BUENO

You have to be confident of your abilities to name your restaurant "All good". But original inhabitants, pre-Spanish times: *Atalayita* (131 D5) (*∅ F9*). Excavations left of the end of the road have uncovered various small igloo-like buildings made from lava rocks, many of which have been restored. It seems to have been a shepherd settlement and the shelters were probably not used as homes but rather as storage rooms and meat drying rooms. From the 15th century rectangular, larger buildings were added, including some shelters for live stock. A small museum opposite the entrance provides information about the excavations. The solidified lava flow (the outflow of the lava field Malpaís Grande) where the goats of the indigenous Canary Island inhabitants roamed, was created by one of the island's last eruptions about ten thousand years ago. On the ☀ summit of the eastern hill, you can look out over the whole terrain.

The fishing village, *Pozo Negro* (131 D5) (*∅ G9*) ("black fountain") consists of little more than two rows of houses on a bay with a black pebble and dark sand beach. There are two lovely restaurants with sea views that serve fresh fish (*Budget*).

SAVIMAX (129 E3) (*∅ E8*)

On this aloe vera plantation you can see this age-old medicinal plant up close, also on sale at the factory are the products that are derived from it. *At the roundabout on the FV 50 go 5 km/3 miles in the direction of Valles de Ortega, after 150 m/ 492 ft turn left onto the estate*

TISCAMANITA/MILL MUSEUM (129 D4) (*∅ E9*)

In Tiscamanita, from Antigua on the FV20 10 km/6.2 miles to the south, you can visit the mill museum (*Centro de Interpretación de los Molinos*) which is housed in a restored windmill with adjoining farm buildings. It has a well-preserved collection that provides insights into Fuerteventura's tradition-rich milling trade and millrighting history. Every guest receives a complimentary sample of *gofio*. *Tue–Sat 10am–6pm | admission 2 euros | coming from Antigua, turn right uphill in the left turn when you enter the village*

TRIQUIVIJATE (130 C2–3) (*∅ F7*)

This little hamlet east of Antigua would not be worth the visit if it was not for the fine restaurant *Antonia (Piedra Blanca 146 | tel. 6 44 14 71 57 | antoniatriquivijate. com | Expensive)*. It opens only if you pre-book. Master chef Kira Schilling will tell you the daily specialities on the phone. You dine in a lovely courtyard or an elegant living room. You can't get more individual than that!

★ **Betancuria**
Church, cloister, and crafts – Fuerteventura's history lives on in this old mountain village
→ p. 58

★ **Barranco de las Peñitas**
Hike along the dam and down an isolated and rocky gorge
→ p. 60

★ **Pájara's parish church**
Village church with the famous Mexican baroque portal
→ p. 66

★ **Oasis Park**
Take time out from the beach and spend an interesting day at the cactus garden and zoo
→ p. 69

MARCO POLO HIGHLIGHTS

BETANCURIA

(129 D3) *(Ø D7)* **This is the most historic town on the island.** ★ ● **Betancuria was founded in 1405 by the Norman Jean de Béthencourt, who had conquered the island in the name of the Castilian crown.**

The little village (700 inhabitants) can only be reached via winding mountain roads. It is very pretty with a number of restored old mansions. Life here is influenced by tourism today. *Park at the southern village entrance, then walk to the church*

SIGHTSEEING

CASA SANTA MARÍA

The most beautiful features of the island are shown here, and not just in the main attraction, the amazing ● INSIDER TIP multi-media show and the 3D cinema with underwater footage *(last shows 3:15pm)*. The historical photos and farming equipment as well as an embroidery demonstration are also very interesting; linger in the peaceful shaded garden. *Mon–Sat 10am–3:30pm | admission 6 euros | entrance past the restaurant with the same name | www.casasantamaria. net*

CONVENTO DE SAN BUENAVENTURA

In the valley before the northern entrance of the town are the ruins of a 17th century Franciscan monastery. Since the secularization of the monastery in 1836, the citizens have used the site as a stone quarry which is why the cloister is gone. Opposite the church is a chapel. It was built in front of a cave where, during the 15th century, San Diego (a miracle worker and missionary) was believed to have lived.

IGLESIA DE SANTA MARÍA

The current church that towers over the valley floor was built in 1620 as a replacement to the first cathedral which was destroyed by pirates in 1593. The triple-naved church is built in the island's typical Mudéjar style (with wooden ceilings) and contains a number of altars. Amongst them a beautiful baroque main altar that dates back to 1684. In the left niche of the altar on the southern wall (to the right of the entrance when seen from the inside) is a wood carved statue of Santa Catalina. It is regarded as one of the oldest surviving works of art on the island. The sacristy *(entrance left of the altar room)* with its carved and painted wooden ceiling is another attraction. *Mon–Sat 10am–12:30pm, 1pm–3:50pm, Sun 10:30am–2:20pm | admission 1.50 euros*

MUSEO ARQUEOLÓGICO

The museum is on the main road and is guarded by two cannons that were captured from English pirates in 1740 during the Battle of Tamacite. Inside, displays of photos and texts tell the history of the indigenous population and their culture. *Mon–Sat 10am–6pm | admission 2 euros | on the main road*

FOOD & DRINK

For a snack, go to the *Casa Santa María cafeteria (Plaza Santa Maria 1 | access from below | Budget)*, which serves drinks and homemade cake in a separate part of the garden. *Don Carmelo (between Casa Sana María and the road)* pleases his guests with tapas in a Canarian setting.

INSIDER TIP CASA SANTA MARÍA

The Casa Santa María: an award-winning restaurant that is stylish without being over-the-top. Particularly the two inner courtyards are a sheer delight. The kitchen serves sophisticated Canarian dishes. *Mon–Sat 10am–6pm, closed May | at the church square | tel. 928 87 82 82 | www. casasantamaria.net | Expensive*

SHOPPING

In various shops close to the church – especially at the *Casa Santa María* – you will find the island's best and most varied range of arts and crafts on sale. The items are from all over the island and include culinary delights such as prickly pear jam and jars of ready-made mojo sauce.

WHERE TO GO

TEGÚ ☼ (129 D3) (*ⓜ D7*)

From the top of the pass at the Tegú mountain (645 m/2,116 ft) north of the town you will get a lovely view of the island's old capital Betancuria, and of the northern part of the island. The viewing point and car park is dominated by two large statues, which represent the ancient Fuerteventura kings (or chiefs) Guise and Ayose – heroic images of rather dubious artistic value. The viewing point ● *Mirador Morro Velosa (Tue–Sat 10am–6pm)* higher up at 640 m/2,100 ft offers even more impressive panoramic views of the landscape as well as a small museum and a café.

VEGA DE RÍO DE LAS PALMAS/ BARRANCO DE LAS PEÑITAS
(128 C 3–4) (*ⓜ C–D8*)

About 6 km/3.7 miles south of Betancuria is probably the island's most beautiful palm tree oasis. The farming settlement is also called *Vega de Río Palma*. The 17th century *village church* on the left hand side *(daily 10:30am– 1pm, 4pm–6pm)* has the most precious

Six hundred years of history: Betancuria

holy object on the island: a 23 cm/9 inch alabaster figurine of the Virgen de la Peña, Virgin Mary with Child. This figure of Mary is thought to be the oldest on the island and was probably brought here from France during the 15th century by the conqueror Jean de Béthencourt. As patron saint of the island, every September the virgin is the destination of the largest pilgrimage on

creek for a second time and park your car. From there you can walk down the valley along the dry river bed towards the reservoir. After 15 minutes, just before the tamarisk forest, leave the river bed to the right (just after another distinctive track that also turns right) and continue above the forest and then along the silted-up *Embalse de las Peñitas* reservoir. After about 10–15 min-

The goal of every hike through the Barranco de las Peñitas is the Ermita de la Peña

the island. At the church square, the fine delicatessen and restaurant *Don Antonio* is a great place to recharge.

From the southern end of the oasis you can go on one of the most beautiful hikes that the island has to offer to the rocky ★ *Barranco de las Peñitas* gorge. Drive 400 m/1,300 ft towards Pájara, as the main road starts to climb, take a right turn into the valley at Vega de Río Palma (signposted) and go a further 1,300 m where the road crosses the

utes you will reach the dam. Just beyond it the path leads down through two bends to the dramatic rocky gorge.

After a few minutes you will reach the whitewashed *Ermita de la Peña* chapel, a cool, peaceful place of rest. When the wind blows through the rocks here it makes some rather eerie sounds, like the whispers of a ghostly choir! To return you backtrack on the same path. The whole hike should take about 90 minutes (including a bit of a break). At some places you will need to be very sure-footed and don't forget to take some water! Back at the starting point of the hike, treat yourself to a visit to a place that makes both body and soul happy; the *Casa de la Naturaleza (Mon–Sat 10am–5pm)* with its exhibition on the animal and plant world (excellent photos and multi-media show), a cafeteria *(Moderate)* and a beautiful, paradisiacal Canarian atmosphere.

GOAT FARM ●
(129 D3) *(∅ D7)*

Goats are everywhere! From the *Finca de Pepe* car park go right through the goat stables (among much bleating) to the cheese factory, where you can see how the cheeses are produced and where you can also buy a selection of goat's cheese and other goat's milk products. *From the FV 30 opposite the monastery ruins 1.6 km/1 mile uphill*

CALETA DE FUSTES

(131 E3) *(∅ G8)* **The holiday resort Caleta de Fustes has been developed since 1980 and lies on a gently curved south facing bay on the island's east coast, just 7 km/4.5 miles south of the airport.**

It is very popular with British holidaymakers. In brochures, maps and on signs it is also referred to as Costa Caleta, Playa de Castillo, Castillo de Fuste or El Castillo. The "castillo" refers to the *Castillo de Fustes*, a round stone tower that was built in 1740 as the town's defence against pirates. Today it forms a decorative part of the bungalow hotel complex, *Barceló Castillo Beach Resort*.

SIGHTSEEING

DREAMS HOUSE MUSEUM
A dream for any collector: an entire factory building housing all types of different models: ships, aeroplanes, doll's houses, fantasy figures, trains and much more – a spectacular attraction! *Tue–Sun 10am–6pm | admission 6 euros | 2.5 km/1.5 miles to the north (turn right at Ikea) | dreamshousemuseum.es*

FOOD & DRINK

Nothing on the island compares to the stylish gastronomy on the harbour, characterised by its contemporary, elegant ambience and white décor as well as excellent sea-views throughout. Up in the harbour building (with terrace) you can eat in the buffet restaurant *La Ancla (evenings only | Expensive)*, while the ground floor houses the à-la-carte restaurant *El Camarote (Moderate)*, the ice-cream parlour *La Goleta* and the bar *Noray*. At the front of the pier, the lounge bar *El Faro (daily 10am–1am)* with its panoramic view completes the excellent choice on offer here. You can eat inside or outside at any one of the bars or restaurants *(tel. for all: 928 16 31 00)*.

The town itself also offers a wide selection of bars but without a sea view. *La Perlita* to the north-east of the beach, the Beach Café at the hotel *Geranios* (both providing snacks only) and the pleasant beach bar `INSIDERTIP` *La Isla (Moderate)* to the south all offer views out to sea. The latter one is on a man-made island in the south of the bay and can only be reached via a bridge, they also serve meals. *El Capitán (opposite the Barceló Fuerteventura | tel. 928 16 37 23 | Budget–Moderate)* is a very popular tapas bar with Canarian atmosphere, a palm tree terrace and live music.

SHOPPING

Shopping centres are dotted all over the island; the largest of them is *CC Atlántico* in the south offering the widest selection of goods (clothing, sport items, food, and electronic goods), all shops being fully air-conditioned. Most shoppers come here for the bargain prices at the large supermarket *Eurospar Padilla*. Fun and excitement can be had at the ● *Family Entertainment Center*, with its many restaurants – an ideal hangout for rainy days. Saturday is market day *(9am–2pm | in the west close to the road)* where you can pick up wood carvings, clothing, jewellery and much more besides.

SPORTS & ACTIVITIES

From the town you can either head up into the mountains or down into the sea. Explore the island's inland and coastline on two (three or four) wheels or go scuba-diving; both should be high on your list of priorities if you're of the adventurous type.

BOAT TOURS

Oceanarium in the harbour offers a range of activities from dolphin and whale watching boat trips, semi-submarine tours to explore the underwater world and deep sea fishing (see below). The large catamaran *Oby Cat (tel. 6 36 59 55 81 | www.obycat.com)* is also anchored at the harbour waiting to take passengers to the bay of Pozo Negro for a spot of snorkelling followed by a steaming paella to be enjoyed on board.

BIKES, BUGGIES, TRIKES

The island's rugged volcanic landscape is at your doorstep waiting to be explored. How you choose to explore your surroundings is entirely up to you. Originally from England, affable Geoff owns *Caleta Cycles (at the beachside Hotel Geranios | tel. 6 76 60 01 90).* and takes guests on guided bike tours. He also has a wide selection of rental bikes for all types. *Castillo Tour (also called Fuertesafari | tel. 6 26 33 31 43)* organises buggy safaris while motorbikes and bicycles are available to hire from *East Coast Rides (tel. 6 93 24 92 45 | www.east coastrides.es)*. A cheaper alternative for electric scooters and other vehicles is *Excursiones La Guirra (at the beachside Hotel Geranios | tel. 6 76 31 92 42)*. However the real hit, especially for couples, are the organised INSIDER TIP chauffeur-driven trike tours, for example by *Cool Runnings (CC El Castillo | on the car park side | tel. 6 49 93 85 81 | www.fuertetrikes.com)*.

GOLF

South of the town there are two 18-hole golf courses next to each other: the *Fuerteventura Golf Club (tel. 9 28 16 00 34 | www.fuerteventuragolfclub.com)* and the *Golf Club Salinas de Antigua (tel. 9 28 87 72 72 | www.salinasgolf.com)*. The former is also the older and larger of the two with long stretches, but both are par 70 and have views of the Atlantic.

OCEANARIUM

A popular destination for everyone, offering boat trips (see above) as well as kayak and peddle boat hire, jet skiing, jet packing or flyboarding and even swimming with sea lions. Children have a great time playing on the inflatable water play area. *In the harbour area | tel. 9 28 54 76 87 | www.oceanariumexplorer.com*

WATER SPORTS

Let's start with diving: the diving school *Deep Blue (tel. 9 28 16 37 12 | www.deepblue-diving.com)* with its ideal location at the harbour. Volker and his team know

Why wait? The windsurfing boards are lined up ready on the beach Caleta de Fustes

the best diving spots to be reached by boat from their own jetty. They take you to see ● fantastic underwater lava formations where you can spot shoals of brightly coloured fish hiding in the crevices and caves – an amazing 3D cinematic experience. The resort would not be complete without a surfing centre: *Canary Surf Academy (at the beachside Hotel Geranios | tel. 6 47 93 06 08)*. The bay is particularly suitable for beginners (and for SUP).

ENTERTAINMENT

A show or live music can be enjoyed every evening at *Piero's (CC El Castillo | www.pieroscafe.com)* – pleasant also because it's half open. The *Beach Café (until 11pm | Hotel Geranios | at the westerly point of the beach)* shakes up cocktails with a sea view. Unsurpassed are

the bars directly on the harbour where *El Faro* doesn't close until after midnight.

WHERE TO STAY

BARCELÓ CASTILLO BEACH RESORT

This large complex consists of 390 apartments and bungalows – all with their own balcony or terrace – and is situated directly on the beach. It has a large seawater swimming pool area grouped around the old defence tower. Also freshwater pools (heated in winter), restaurants, shops, tennis courts and entertainment. *Tel. 9 28 16 31 00 | www. barcelo. com | Moderate*

BARCELÓ FUERTEVENTURA ●

All your needs will be catered to here: Caribbean flair, sea views from all 462 rooms, direct beach access, huge pools, mini golf, tennis, saunas, thalasso spa, entertainment for young and old and many other pleasures. *Tel. 9 28 54 75 17 | www.barcelo.com | Moderate–Expensive*

BRONCEMAR BEACH
Looking for low-budget accommodation yet still close to the beach? Then you have come to the right address. It is not a spacious complex and the apartments facing the street can be noisy yet it has everything you need including three (!) swimming pools. *252 apartments | C/ Ajican 4 | tel. 9 28 16 39 33 | www.broncemar-beach. com | Budget*

There is seldom a crowd on the harbour promenade at Las Playitas

INFORMATION
OFICINA DE TURISMO
West of CC Centro Castillo | tel. 9 28 16 32 86

WHERE TO GO

SALINAS DEL CARMEN AND PUERTO DE LA TORRE (131 E4) *(𝄚 G8–9)*
3 km/2 miles south of Caleta de Fustes you turn left to the *Salinas del Carmen* salt pans, the core of the *Salt Museum (Tue–Sat 10am–6pm | admission 5 euros)*. The road leads directly up to the entrance and the visitor's centre which you should visit first before walking through the salt pans. For demonstration purposes the salt pans are still operated in the traditional manner. Down in the village, INSIDER TIP *Los Caracolitos (closed Wed | tel. 9 28 17 42 42 | Budget)* has made a name for itself as one of the best fish restaurants in the area.

LAS PLAYITAS

(135 E4–5) *(𝄚 E11)* **The name Las Playitas, "the little beaches", refers to the peaceful fishing village at the end of the road.**
The larger of the small beaches is separated from the village by a hill and has been developed into a holiday destination mainly for families and sports enthusiasts. In the picturesque old village with its whitewashed cubist houses, visitors and locals alike are attracted by the modest promenade and the small pier.

FOOD & DRINK

LA RAMPA DE TÍO ENRIQUE 〰
Freshly caught fish with a sea view! You can choose from the freshly caught fish which the waiter shows to you at your table. *Closed Tue, closed Mon evenings |*

Av. Miramar 1 | at the pier | tel. 9 28 34 40 04 | Moderate

SPORTS & ACTIVITIES

The *Playitas Grand Resort* is a sports resort geared towards both amateurs and professionals and it has an Olympic sized swimming pool. Other facilities include tennis courts, beach volleyball, a large fitness centre, the *Cycle Centre* with bicycle hire and organised bicycle tours, the scuba diving school *Deep Blue (tel. 6 53 51 26 38 | www.deep-blue-diving. com)* and the surf and sailing school *Cat Company (tel. 6 16 6 19 93 13 | www.cat-company.eu)* which also has kayaks and surf ski excursions on offer. The showpiece of the sports resort is its 18 hole golf course. It is open to the public, not just for hotel guests, however, hotel guests do get a discount. They also offer golf lessons for beginners and advanced players (complete courses or hourly, *access on the ast side near the Playitas Hotel | bookings at www.playitas.net*).

WHERE TO STAY

PLAYITAS GRAND RESORT

Everything is close together here: a family and child-friendly aparthotel (210 units) on the western side of the valley and the beach, the more elegant *Playitas Hotel* (223 rooms) opposite as well as the bungalow complex *Villas Playitas*. All three surround the golf course and all hotels have direct beach access. *Tel. 9 28 86 04 00 | www.playitas.net | Moderate–Expensive*

WHERE TO GO

GRAN TARAJAL (135 D5) (*∅ E11*)

This sleepy little port town (pop. 10,000, 5 km/3 miles west of Las Playitas) whose

To honour the island's farming tradition: statue on the promenade at Gran Tarajal

name means "big tamaris" does not have anything special about it. But, if you have been here once, you might be amongst those who keep returning. Before you enter the town you pass a large, airy palm grove, park your car in the centre, linger for a moment and listen to the murmur of the fountain on the shady main square and then walk a little further to the ● broad beach promenade. After your stroll you should take a seat in one of the local restaurants. You can look out over the black sandy beach to the glittering sea and watch the activity on the beach feeling wonderfully at ease...

For a bite to eat – with a panoramic view of the beach – try *Pizza & Pomodoro (Budget)*, the best place on the promenade: cheap and good. The 🌐 *Gran Tarajal* beach is a green flag beach. Green flags are awarded for sustainability, i.e. using environmental standards in the management of the beach.

However, the signature of Gran Tarajal is its street art with INSIDER TIP 32 murals decorating the facades. Some of the creative and often humoristic paintings are several storeys high and most are inspired by maritime themes. They turn the town into an open-air art gallery for you to walk around at leisure.

PUNTA DE LA ENTALLADA
(135 E4) (*ℳ F11*)

At Las Playitas an asphalt road turns off to the east. It leads 6 km/3.7 miles to the south-eastern cape *Punta de la Entallada* which has a picturesque ⚓ lighthouse on its highest point.

LOW BUDGET

A small breakfast with milky coffee sets you back just 3.50 euros at the *Café Gala* in Caleta de Fustes *(CC Atlántico on the ground floor, on the beach side)* while a bottle of cava costs a reasonable 13 euros.

Insider tip for those travelling on a shoestring: take advantage of the happy hour at *Taberna del Capitán* in Caleta de Fustes *(opposite Barceló Fuerteventura)* until 10:30pm selling beer at very low prices.

PÁJARA

(128 C4) (*ℳ C–D9*) **The well-kept hamlet Pájara lies in a deep valley and is surrounded by 600 m/1,968 ft mountains that protect it from the harsh winds and make it green, lush and shady.**

The entire south-west of the island is administered by Pájara and one can sense the prosperity that tourism has brought to the region, for example, in the modern town hall and in the fact that the town has the first public swimming pool on the island.

The small terraced fields on the surrounding slopes still bear witness to the fact that this area was also once intensively cultivated. The largest legacy from that period is the parish church. *Parking space in the barranco below the church and town hall | access from the road to Betancuria*

SIGHTSEEING

PÁJARA PARISH CHURCH ★

The nave of the *Iglesia Nuestra Señora de Regla* was built during the 17th century to the beginning of the 18th century. The church became known for its beautiful Mexican baroque façade with Aztec elements. In addition to the geometric sun patterns it also has snakes, panthers and birds. It was, for a long time, a mystery as to how the stone could have been transported all the way from Mexico to this remote place. Today however, we know that the unknown stonemason must have copied the patterns from an Italian sample book and that neither the stone nor the portal façade came from Mexico.

The dark interior of the church has two naves decorated with a wooden ceiling in the Mudéjar style. The Mudéjar style developed during the 14th/15th century in Spain as a combination of the Moorish and Gothic style and was used for a long time on the island. The beautifully gilded baroque altars were completed in 1785. In the afternoons when the sun shines it seems as if they are lit up by spotlights – thanks to small windows that were built so high up that you cannot see them from the church's interior. Right at the entrance is a machine that turns on real spotlights for 1 euro. *Daily 10am–5pm, often shorter*

Daily 11am–4pm | opposite the parking lot below the church | tel. 9 28 16 14 02 | www.casaisaitas.com | Moderate

WHERE TO GO

AJUY (PUERTO DE LA PEÑA)
(128 B3) *(𝄞 C8)*

This fishing village with the two names is a popular sightseeing destination. Electricity and running water were only introduced in 1986. Those in need of some sustenance should go to the

Hiking trail with a sea view at Ajuy/Puerto de la Peña

FOOD & DRINK

INSIDER TIP ▸ CASA ISAÍTAS

Careful restoration work transformed this 200-year-old ruined manor house into a real gem: an intimate four-roomed guesthouse *(Expensive)* with two beautiful inner courtyards and an atmospheric, good restaurant that is famous for its choice of delicious tapas.

"golden cage", the *Jaula de Oro (Moderate)*. Its prime location, directly on the beach, is reflected in its prices and service. A more affordable alternative is *Casa Pepin (Budget)* higher up on the slope but still with a lovely sea view from the terrace. In the same street (above the car park) is the *Trecepeces Shop* selling pretty arts and crafts as well as souvenirs. Puerto de la Peña is also the starting point of two short hikes. On the north end of the beach the hike leads like a ramp over an almost white rocky plateau to the *Caleta Negra* bay where enormous caves have been eroded by the action of the sea. Walk across the plateau to the north, past the old lime kilns (two small gorges below) and follow the signposts "Caleta Negra" to the steep downhill steps. You find yourself in the larger of the two "pirate caves'. The second cave is just next to it. Both are private property, and you might have to pay an entrance fee.

A second destination is the impressive **INSIDER TIP** rock arch that rises at the mouth of the *Barranco de la Peña* north of Ajuy. You reach it by following the road

that branches off above the lime kilns at the highest point that leads to the cave, continue above the Caleta Negra, then go inland up to the next path running north to the *barranco* then turn left. In front of the rock arch is a natural swimming pool, perfect to cool off in.

TUINEJE
(129 D5) (*D–E9*)

The village Tuineje is the Cinderella amongst the old island communities. Tomatoes are grown under protective sun shades (thus reducing the amount of water needed to irrigate them). They are also sorted and packed here. The only place of note – which is more an oddity – is a depiction in the *San Miguel*

A prickly yet picturesque landscape: the cactus garden in Oasis Park at La Lajita

parish church (late 18th century). There, two panels at the base of the altar show the glorious battle of Tamacite, in which a heroic bunch of 37 farmers under the command of the island's captain managed to chase away a troupe of British buccaneers. The key to the church can be obtained in the house opposite the church's west side, the one that has a rather striking commemorative plaque for a pious nun. *10 km/6.2 miles southeast of Pájara*

TARAJALEJO

(134 B5) (*ɶ C12*) On a long black pebble beach on the southern coast, the simple holiday complex Tarajalejo was developed next to a small, plain fishing village.

With just one holiday complex in the entire place, this is a relaxing, low-key resort boasting a long stretch (1 km/0.6 mile) of beach which you might have all for yourself.

FOOD & DRINK

LA BARRACA
Dine on a terrace that is right on the beach. Very simple and also very affordable. Good coffee. *Closed Tue | C/ Isidro Díaz 14 | tel. 9 28 16 10 89 | Budget*

SPORTS & ACTIVITIES

The windsurf center *Watersports-Fuerteventura (tel. 9 28 87 51 10 | water sports-fuerteventura.com)* on the beach side of the hotel also offers catamaran sailing, kayaking, surfing and snorkelling and bicycle hire. *Autos Rent (C/ La Marisma | tel. 9 28 54 71 53)* arranges quad tours and tours with the lowered "buggys". A branch of the *Ocean World*

(C/ Isidro Diaz 14E | tel. 9 28 87 54 44 | www.oceanworld.com) diving schools completes the range of activities on offer.

WHERE TO STAY

BAHÍA PLAYA
A pedestrianised promenade is all that separates this modern, adults-only hotel from the beach. Of the 163 rooms, 79 are spacious junior suites. Three swimming pools and entertainment. *Tel. 9 28 16 10 01 | www.r2hotels.com | Moderate*

WHERE TO GO

OASIS PARK ★
(133 B5) (*ɶ C12*)
What started out as a sad zoo in the 1990s has evolved into one of the main attractions on the island – after the beaches. Here you can enjoy yourself all day long, and if you come back a year later you will be amazed what has been added as the park is constantly expanding and reinventing itself. The nucleus, the zoo, is a spacious shady park with tall trees and flowering shrubs. The main attractions are the very funny **INSIDER TIP** parrot show and three open-air theatres, one each for reptiles, birds of prey and brilliantly trained seals. A new attraction is the opportunity for an up-close meeting with lemurs. An open bus travels around the 40 acres of cactus garden which has over 2,000 plant species and the birds of prey theatre. On offer are several outdoor cafés, a nursery, a well-stocked home and garden shop and the popular camel safaris up to a viewpoint on a dune. *For times and prices see "Travel with kids" (p. 109) | on the FV 2 near La Lajita (2 times daily free buses from all holiday resort towns)*

THE SOUTH

This is the picture book part of Fuerte-ventura – nothing but sun, sand and sea. On the 20 km/12 mile stretch of Playas de Sotavento's beaches you can enjoy sea views from (almost) all the hotel room windows. Out on the waves the sails of the windsurfers add bright splashes of colour. Even at the largest holiday resorts – like the Costa Calma in the northeast and Morro Jable/Jandía Playa in the south – the beaches are never crowded and there is always plenty of space.

Everywhere along this coast the surf is gentle and although there is a constant wind, it is seldom unpleasant. On the Costa Calma and at the lagoons of Playa Barca the wind is generally stronger. Further south the mountains temper the breeze a little bit.

The area was first discovered as a tourist destination by a few Germans, who established the first holiday accommodation in Morro Jable with the still present *Casa Atlántica* and successfully brought the area's pristine beaches to the attention of two German tour operators. Shortly after that, in 1970, the very first Robinson Club was established in one of the first hotels. The name was very apt, because apart from tiny Morro Jable, the Jandía peninsula was almost entirely deserted back then.

The Playas de Sotavento is only one side – actually just a half – of the coin, because the Jandía peninsula stretches beyond the southern cape at Morro Jable another 17 km/10.5 miles to the west, and on the other side is the elongated, re-

Bungalows and bathing fun on the one side and the isolated open spaces of the Jandía peninsula on the other

mote north-west coast. A trip in an off-road vehicle to these long, sandy and wonderfully isolated beaches is one of the highlights of a holiday on Fuerteventura. Between the two coasts is mountain country with *Pico de Jandía* the island's highest cloud covered peak at 807 m/2,647.6 ft.

Even today most of Jandía remains deserted. Because of its ecological importance the whole peninsula has been declared a natural park (with the excep-

tion of the inhabited coastal regions). Especially in the area of the Istmo de la Pared with its massive wind farm, tall fences have been put up to keep out the voracious goats and to give the vegetation a chance to grow.

COSTA CALMA

(133 F4) *(⫴ B12)* **Costa Calma, the "calm coast", refers to the wide holiday**

Lots of sand and sun:
beach at the Costa Calma

zone on the Istmo de la Pared at the beginning of the Jandía peninsula. Here, you can hear German spoken in many places.

This part that lies furthest east is also known as Cañada del Río. The flat terrain on both sides of the main road has allowed – and still allows – building and over the years many bungalow and apartment complexes have sprung up. In between them are also some larger hotels but they are relatively unobtrusive (visually) and the rather unexpectedly

lush green forest alongside the country road is what makes the biggest impression.

Costa Palma is spread out and there is no real village centre. Between the scattered holiday zones there are sections of fallow lands. Yet as a guest, you will not want for anything. After all what more do you need than the sun, a sandy beach and clear water? The sea front that stretches out for miles can sometimes be a bit crowded, yet the beaches stay pristine – obviously the guests also do their bit not to litter – and the water is, like everywhere on the island, of exceptional quality.

FOOD & DRINK

This may come as bad news to frequent visitors to the island but most of the town's best and most popular bars had to close at once when a whole row of houses was knocked down at the end of 2016. Some tourists have found a new regular haunt, for example near the small shopping and eating complexes *Internacional, Plaza* and *Palmeral* at the top end of the old road near the petrol station. A traditional favourite Fuerte action is housed on the ground floor of *CC Palmeral* where you can hang out all day from breakfast until supper tasting your way through their selection of juices, coffees, cocktails and snacks. Practically in the same complex, just one floor above (*CC Plaza),* is *Kapé,* the place for coffee aficionados: the coffee beans are freshly roasted and the cake and snacks are also extremely tasty.

Two local mainstays are the Italian restaurants in *CC Costa Calma:* the slightly less expensive *Mamma mia (Budget)* and the more upmarket *Arena (Budget–Moderate).* From there, cross the road and on the south side of *CC Bahía Calma* is *Rapa Nui,* a popular surfers' café serving breakfast, tapas, nachos, baguettes, cake and cocktails from morning till night. The best chiringuitos – beach bar – is definitely *Aurelia* thanks to regular live music sessions and a wind-sheltered children's play area. Ice cream is available at the Italian-owned *Casa Nostra* on the top floor in *CC Botánico* or *Eisdealer,* 100 m/328 ft along the main road from CC Bahía Calma.

TASCA DOS JOTAS

It is a matter of opinion whether this should be the town's only restaurant worth a mention here. This fine-dining Spanish-Canarian restaurant with white linen tablecloths makes a refreshing change from the town's run-of-the-mill pizzerias, snack bars and surfer bars. The establishment's speciality is goat and goat kids. *Closed Mon | CC Palmeral, upper floor | tel. 9 28 87 51 06 | Moderate– Expensive*

There are seven mostly small shopping centres spread through the holiday zone. The largest supermarket is in the new *CC Bahía Calma* while the shops in the *CC Sotavento (opposite the Hotel Taro Beach)* stock the largest range of wristwatches, jewellery, cosmetics and sunglasses. The *CC El Palmeral* close to the petrol station is the most interesting with shops like *Freestyle* (sportswear), or the surf shop *Fuerte Action,* and the great jewellery shop *1. Stone.*
In the INSIDER TIP *Boutique Tangente (in the hotel Costa Palma Palace, one floor below reception)* Bea Stein, who has been living on the island for years, sells original ready to wear clothing collections, even in larger sizes. Ask about her fashion shows.

The mainly African market that travels around the island in weekly cycles comes to Costa Calma on Wednesdays and Sundays *(9am–2pm | at the lower large roundabout).*

BICYCLE/MOTORBIKE

Volcano Bike (tel. 6 39 73 87 43, Ralph | www.volcano-bike.com) will deliver a mountain bike to your hotel for you, they also offer guided tours from easy to sweaty. Off-road dirt bike tours are offered by *Sahara Sports (tel. 6 69 79 71 62, Frank | www.enduro-guru.com).* *Xtreme (at the Hotel Taro Beach | tel. 9 28 87 56 30| www.xtreme-car-rental. com)* offers quad, trike and buggy tours, hires out bicycles with and without motor, finds sailing, fishing and jet ski trips. Whether with motor or muscle power: do not miss out on the INSIDER TIP guided tours.

MARCO POLO HIGHLIGHTS

★ **Playa Barca**
South of Costa Calma the wind, sand and waves have created an endless beach → p. 78

★ **Dunes at Risco del Paso**
Sand dunes and secluded little hollows at the southern end of the lagoon → p. 81

★ **Pico de la Zarza**
Can only be reached on foot: Fuerte's highest summit → p. 88

★ **Western cape and Cofete**
An amazing vantage point, isolated beaches where you can experience the island's raw nature → p. 89

JET SKI, WATERSKI

And a lot more besides: peddle boats, banana boats (and "hot dogs" suitable for children), kayaks, water skis and all kinds of water sports are on offer at a well-managed station to the north of

SURFING

To try your hand at riding the waves, the best way is to be picked up from your hotel by one of the operators based in La Pared, for example *Waveguru* (see p. 77) as the only suitable waves can be found

Bathing is dangerous in zones designated for surfers and kite surfers

the beach at the hotel *Barlovento (tel. 6 16 43 71 84 | www.excursionesmarytierra.com)*.

SCUBA DIVING

Simona and Kay run *Fuerte Divers* in the Hotel Costa Calma Beach *(second to last hotel before the northern edge of the beach | entrance through the hotel garden | tel. 6 28 01 77 17 | www.fuertedivers.com)*. Not only the nicest diving instructors imaginable, they also take excellent care of their guests. The couple make their dives more exciting with sunken wrecks and by creating their own underwater biotopes made from specially designed frames to entice diverse sea life. Divers are transported to the diving spots in powerful, motorised dinghies.

on the west coast of Fuerteventura. In Costa Calma, contact *Rapa Nui (CC Bahia Calma | tel. 9 28 54 91 40 | www.rapanui-surfschool.com)*, the surf school with the café bar of the same name.

TOURS

Prickly pears are a delicious fruit yet a nightmare to peel if you don't have the knack. Learn how to master the art by taking one of Kristina's excellent tours in the island's south: Her *tapas tour* takes you to an olive plantation and a cheese dairy. Or visit one of the island's wineries to taste Fuerteventura wine accompanied with snacks on the *volcano and wine tour*. *Wild coasts & legends* takes you to the rugged west coast. It's important to book well in advance because Kristina's minivan only has room for si guests. *Tel. 6 17 69 40 67 | fuerte-authen tic-tours.com*

WINDSURFING

The epitome of the Fuerteventura feeling! Wind and kite surfers from around the world flock to the paradise setting of Playa Barca (129 E4) (*ω B12*), for the strong gusts of wind which sweep through the mountains, for its expansive lagoon in tune with the rhythm of the tides and for its landscape dominated exclusively by sand, sea and skies. The first to discover the region's potential was René Egli in 1984 when he opened his own surf station here. It soon became the largest on the island and known worldwide for the surfer's world cup held here regularly in June. René Egli's *kitesurf station (tel. 9 28 54 74 83 | www.rene-egli.com)* lies directly below Hotel *Meliá Gorriones,* the windsurfing centre is approx. 200 m/656 ft away in the direction of Costa Calma. The latest craze is land sailing along the beaches.

Or do you prefer quieter, low key alternatives and shorter distances? Then surf with *Ion Club (tel. 6 61 34 96 89 | www. ionclubfuerte.com)* at Costa Calma beach (between *Costa Calma Palace* and *Monica Beach Hotel).* The kite surfing station in Risco del Paso also belongs to the club – a fantastic location at the south end of the large lagoon. The centre provides transport.

ENTERTAINMENT

Dancing, drinking, chilling out – there's no better place for doing that than on the upper level of the *CC Bahía Calma,* and not only on weekends. This is ensured by no less than three prominent cocktail bars and clubs: *Los Piratas* (sounds like an outmoded place with pirate dec-

orations, but this is far from true), *B-Side* (things really get going from midnight onwards) and the INSIDER TIP *DVN*. This is an abbreviation of "Divino", divine, and this club/bar with billiards and shishas on offer is no less likable than its equally divine predecessor which had to be torn down.

Then there's the *San Borondón* at the *CC Sotavento*. Because of the hams hanging from the ceiling, you might at first suspect a folkloristic tourist trap. Fittingly, Felix, the proprietor, sometimes sings and plays guitar. But maybe you should wait until his son Ari stops waiting tables and starts singing Beatles classics on stage. On Saturday nights, he even performs with his band, which thrills the audience with emotional soul and intoxicating rock.

WHERE TO STAY

APARTAMENTOS MORASOL

Good choice for those on a shoestring budget. Its beachfront location and apartments with sea view are great value for money. One tip is to book the self-catering option and to dine regularly in the resort's restaurants. *36 apartments | C/ Baja de*

LOW BUDGET

All the scuba diving schools offer free trial lessons and even though they only take place in the hotel pool, they are enough to give you an idea of how it is done.

Until 6pm, the pizzeria *Mamma mia (at the CC Costa Calma)* offers a three-course menu of the day for 9.99 euros -- drink included!.

los Erizos | tel. 9 28 54 70 89 | www.mora solhoteles.es | Budget

BAHÍA CALMA BEACH
Beautiful, close to the beach and yet still affordable – which makes it unparalleled in the village.. The bright white, cleverly designed and, for the most part, refurbished 120 bungalows, studios and apartments are grouped around a pool; the beach, restaurants and two shopping centres are all close by. At night the rustle of the palm trees will send you off to sleep. Tel. 9 28 54 71 58 | Moderate

COSTA CALMA PALACE
This is truly a palace – a four star hotel that is 300 m/984 ft long, has up to nine storeys, a massive lobby and dominates the area. The guests – mostly adults wanting to get away from it all for some peace and quiet – enjoy sea views from all the 370 rooms, breakfast underneath the palm trees and a comprehensive spa programme with salt water swimming pools and thalasso therapy. There are two tennis courts and a golf practice facility. Av. Jahn Reisen | tel. 9 28 87 60 10 | www.sbhfue.com | Expensive

MARYVENT
This is a complex of 45 self-catering apartments (in different sizes) that is located right on the beach and is spread over three storeys. Each apartment has its own kitchen and balcony (or terrace) and most have sea views. Below the shopping centre Bahía Calma | tel. 9 28 54 73 92 | www.maryvent.com | Moderate

MELIÁ GORRIONES (129 D5) (𝜚 A13)
Its wonderful location, far from other hotels in a nature reserve just above the lagoon of the Playa Barca, makes it quite special. The interior of the 418 room hotel (they also have spacious family rooms) is quite tasteful. As soon as you enter the reception area you will be impressed with its aesthetics. The hotel has he Egli surf school. Another attraction is the large shady garden with three swimming pools. Entertainment, child care facilities, a spa area and various bars complete the picture. Tel. 9 28 54 70 25 | www.melia.com | Moderate–Expensive

PLAYA ESMERALDA
One of the features of this comfortable, 333 room hotel is the direct access to the beach. It also has good cuisine, affordable prices and an indoor swimming pool for inclement days. At the southern edge of the resort | tel. 9 28 87 53 53 | h10hotels. com | Moderate

RISCO DEL GATO
This small but discerning bungalow hotel (51 units) was seen as an architectural sensation when it opened. Accommodation is in low private bungalows with shell-shaped roofs which protect the intimate sun terraces from the north-east trade winds and from prying eyes. The complex has swimming pools, a sauna, tennis court, cafeteria and restaurant. At the southern edge of the resort | tel. 9 28 54 71 75 | www.vikhotels.com | Expensive

SOTAVENTO BEACH CLUB
Family-friendly resort complex with direct beach access and multiple leisure and (low-key) entertainment possibilities to choose from. Some of the spacious 310 apartments have sea views, they all have terraces or balconies. Scuba diving school on the premises. Don't book all-inclusive here, but rather dine elsewhere sometimes! Tel. 9 28 54 70 60 | www. sotaventobeachclub.com | Moderate

TARO BEACH HOTEL

If it is social mingling you are after, then this is the right place for you. This terraced hotel is directly on the beach. Almost all the 293 rooms have ocean views and private sun terraces. In the centre there is a large swimming pool with ocean view and a shady sunbathing area under palm trees. As usual, there

named after the wall – and it is a place for individualists. Visitors to La Pared either want to stay away from any hustle and bustle, or they want to surf. For the west coast is ideal for surfing – especially at *El Viejo Rey* beach. The oldest of the three surf experts is *Waveguru (tel. 6 19 80 44 47 | www.waveguru.de/en/ surfschool-index.html*). Course partici-

Pool with palms: the Hotel Costa Calma Palace

are quite a number of sports and entertainment possibilities. *Tel. 9 28 54 70 76 | www.sbhfue.com | Moderate*

WHERE TO GO

LA PARED (133 F3) (*Ø B11*)

The narrowest part of the island, the desert-like *Istmo de la Pared* ("isthmus of the wall") is situated at Costa Calma. One theory is that the wall separated two ancient Canarian kingdoms but there is no evidence to support this. The La Pared settlement on the west coast has been

pants can also stay here for free in a surfcamp close to the beach.

The only hotel is the *La Pared (tel. 9 28 86 04 00 | Moderate)*; with just 93 rooms, it is modest in size and also offers sporting facilities. The Canarian restaurant *Bahía La Pared (Moderate)* offers fresh fish and sea views, beautiful at sunset. It lies north of the *barrancos* (ravines) at the end of a path near a rocky outcrop with a section that has been worn by the action of the waves into an arch. During high tide, and if the sea is rough, the seawater surges up and jets through the opening. The beach is a good place to linger: small pools are formed by the tide in the shallow sedimentary rocks, little fish swim in the shallows at low tide, sea worms make strange patterns in the sand and the ochre coloured cliffs, black pebbles and reddish sand form changing patterns and contrasts, and above the rock arch the sea foam evaporates into natural salt pans.

The stables *Rancho Barranco de los Caballos (tel. 6 19 27 53 89)* offers experienced riders INSIDER TIP wonderful rides through the beautiful and isolated terrain on the wild western coast. Drive 20.5 km/12.7 miles on then left on the FV 605 in the direction of Pájara.

Coming from Costa Calma on the country road, do not turn left towards the town, but take a right and follow the dirt road for 1.4 km/0.8 miles to *Quesería La Pastora (Mon–Fri 9am–6:30pm, Sat 9am–2pm)* where you can learn more about the production of goat's cheese and also buy cheese directly from the producers.

MIRADOR DE SOTAVENTO ☼

(134 A–B6) (𝖔 C12)

The *mirador* (viewing point) is primarily a restaurant – and aptly named. Here you can dine outside on a ● covered, wind-protected terrace that has views of the distant coast and the ocean. *Thu–Tue from 1pm | via the old country road in the direction of Matas Blancas, then follow the signs "Mirador" | tel. 6 92 06 65 82 | Moderate*

PLAYA BARCA ★

(133 E4–5, F4) (𝖔 A13/B12)

This middle section of the sandy beaches, with Costa Calma on the northern end, is the most beautiful part of the

Playas de Sotavento. Here, behind a narrow 4 km/2.4 miles long spit of land, is a large lagoon up to 500 m/1,640 ft wide that is dry at low tide or easy to wade through. The spit is sometimes flooded, so be careful that your belongings do not float away! The only large building here is the *Meliá Gorriones* hotel (see p. 76). The Playa Barca is one of the best windsurfing spots in the world and every year in July the world championships take place here.

ESQUINZO/ BUTIHONDO

(133 D6) (𝖔 D3) **From the motorway the Butihondo exit leads to two separate holiday resorts. In the part closer to the**

A symphony of browns and yellows on the wild western coast: beach at La Pared

exit, you can turn left to the Robinson Club or right to several other large hotel complexes.

But if you follow the "Farmacía" sign at the rooundabout, the route takes you via the old road to the older part of *Esqinzo*. Parts of this area are very steep so quite a few of the hotel rooms have sea views. As the road runs above the resort, the area is also very quiet - and even outside of the resort quite peaceful. Buses travel to Morro Jable/ Jandía Playa up to twice an hour from the main country road.

FOOD & DRINK

CASANOVA

The *Sensimar Royal Palm* hotel sells itself as an exclusive, fine-dining establishment. The spacious table setting and first-class service underline its exclusivi-

ty yet the atmosphere is sobering. The Italian inspired cuisine is extremely creative though without losing sight of tradition. Treat yourself to at least two courses followed by a dessert. But if you enjoy a leisurely dinner, the five-course menu is also highly recommended. *Sensimar Royal Palm/last hotel in Butihondo in the direction Morro Jable | tel. 8 28 12 01 50 | Expensive*

INSIDERTIP▶ MARABÚ

Those who work in the tourism industry in the south, take their guests to this establishment. Everything here is spot on: the atmosphere, the service, the value for money as well as the variety and quality of the food. Traditional island dishes, international dishes, fresh ingredients and good wine. There is also a terrace. *Closed Sun | C/ Fuente de Hija | straight down from the country road | tel. 9 28 54 40 98 | e-marabu.com | Expensive*

SPORTS & ACTIVITIES

Below the resorts the long Playa de Esquinzo beach stretches out (many nudist beaches). The *Robinson Club* has the widest choice of activities: apart from tennis, beach volleyball, football and much more, there is also a water sports station for catamaran sailing, windsurfing and SUP. If you are not staying at the club, you can visit *Matchpoint Sports* for all matters concerning tennis *(on artificial grass or clay courts) and for swimming lessons (in the garden of the Fuerteventura Princess | tel. 9 28 54 43 07)*. The latest craze is mermaid swimming where both legs are squeezed inside a fabric tail fin!

ENTERTAINMENT

In the old part of Esquinzo, the meeting place is *Safari Bar* at the Monte del Mar swimming pool. The *Caretta Beach* bar located below the *Jandia Princess Club* is a popular venue playing live music and only closes at midnight.

WHERE TO STAY

ESQUINZO/MONTE DEL MAR
The two neighbouring complexes are under the same management. Both are close to the beach and both have a small swimming pool. The *Monte del Mar* even has a small shop and the popular *Safari Bar*. *140 units | C/ Escanfraga 2 | tel. 9 28 54 40 75 | info@canariaturistica.eu | Moderate*

FUERTEVENTURA PRINCESS/
CLUB JANDÍA PRINCESS
The two four star resort complexes each comprise of one large main hotel, two-storey units scattered in a garden and a pool area with restaurants and bars. Both impress with their traditional island style with white walls and dark wood. The main building of the *Fuerteventura Princess* hotel with its huge lobby is an architectural revelation. The *Jandía Princes*s, which is run as an all-inclusive club with one adults-only area and another area for families, has 528 air-conditioned rooms and the *Fuerteventura Princess* has 715, all with telephone and private balcony or terrace, often with sea views. They also offer tennis courts, a sauna, entertainment and direct beach access. *Fuerteventura Princess: tel. 9 28 54 41 36 | Expensive | Jandía Princess: tel. 9 28 54 40 89 | Expensive | both: www.princess-hotels.com*

ROBINSON CLUB ESQUINZO PLAYA
The newer of the island's two Robinson Clubs can accommodate 1,000 guests with a focus on families. Their entertainment and child care facilities are ideal and one part of the resort complex is a quiet resting zone. Highlights include the wide choice of treatments and sporting activities as well as direct (albeit steep) access to the beach. *Tel. 9 28 16 80 00 | www.robinson.com | Expensive*

SENSIMAR ROYAL PALM
This high-end newcomer among the hotels in the south appeals because of its extravagance, first-class cuisine (four restaurants) and its location above the beach. Its Italian inspired architecture is also attractive. All of the 334 rooms open up onto spacious balconies or patios. Bed and breakfast is definitely recommended due to its secluded location away from restaurants and bars. Unfortunately children are not welcome... *In the very west of Butihondo | tel. 8 28 12 01 50 | www.royalpalmfuerteventura.com | Expensive*

WHERE TO GO

VIEWPOINT AT BARRANCO DE LOS CANARIOS ☆ (133 E5) (𝒲 D2)

Instead of driving along the motorway to Costa Calma, take the old road and head down into the valley at the petrol station. After approx. 6 km/3.7 miles where the road comes to an end, the panoramic landscape suddenly opens out in front of you. The desolate northern coast stretches westward umtil it reaches Punta Pesebre 15.6 km/10 miles away. Cofete can also be spotted on the slope. However the mysterious Villa Winter is hidden behind a ridge in the terrain.

DUNES AT RISCO DEL PASO ★
(133 E5) (𝒲 A13)

At Risco del Paso (turn off the country road on to an asphalt road at 71.8 km/45 miles) the Playa Barca lagoon ends. The attractions of this little stretch of beach – one of the most beautiful on the island –

are its two small sand dunes and its grassy knolls and secluded little hollows. Quite a number of nudists. The sea in front of Risco del Paso is a favourite surf spot with a branch of the *Ion Club* windsurf station from Costa Calma.

MORRO JABLE/JANDÍA PLAYA

(132–133 C–D6) (𝒲 C–D3) **The double village Morro Jable/Jandia Playa at the most southern tip of Fuerteventura forms the largest tourist centre on the island. It consists of two very different parts.**

Morro Jable (or Morro del Jable) is a not very old yet traditional harbour village in a beautiful location. East of it, on the other side of a hill, which is now almost

Show of flowers along the harbour promenade at Morro Jable

completely built up, hotels and apartment complexes make up the large holiday resorts that have come to be known as Jandía Playa or Jandía. The official names are *Solana de Matorral* or *Solana de Jandía*. Its beach is the *Playa de Matorral*.

Jandía Playa essentially consists of a prestigiously laid-out, leafy main road parallel to the coast with terraced hotel and

Never far from the sea:
restaurant in Morro Jable

apartment complexes built down the slope on its one side, extending far and wide. Here there are numerous bars, restaurants and shops. So much so that by now a lively promenade has developed, linking the hotel *Labranda World* (the former *Stella Canaris)* in the east with the

old, clunky *Cosmo* shopping centre in the west. The promenade is particularly busy at night. A protected salt marsh stretches along the other side of the road; behind it lies the beach.

The beach promenade which starts at the Robinson Club and leads up to Morro Jable and the popular fish restaurants is smaller, quieter, more atmospheric and nearer the water. The simplicity and authentic Spanish nature of the old part of Morro Jable offers an interesting contrast to the artificial, large-scale holiday resorts in its immediate neighbourhood.

SIGHTSEEING

A sea turtle preservation station is situated at the harbour where you can watch the turtles swimming in the pool *(Mon–Fri 10am–1pm | to the right in front of the harbour gate)*. At the restaurant run by the fishers' cooperative *(Cofradía),* swarms of fish can be seen in the basin and with a bit of luck, you may catch a glimpse of rays skimming through the water.

FOOD & DRINK

If you do not mind the trip, then you can have a lovely intimate lunch (or dinner) in Morro Jable. There on the beach promenade you will be able to dine better than at the restaurants on the main road at Jandía Playa. The restaurants all offer a very similar menu choice and the quality and standards are all on par with each other. Recommended is the solid *Saavedra Clavijo (daily | tel. 9 28 16 60 80 | Moderate)*. If you prefer to eat well and don't mind missing out on the sea view, try the restaurants in the second row behind the promenade, where you can dine better and/or cheaper, eg.g. at *Charly (Plaza Cirilo López 1 | tel. 9 28 54 10 66 | Moderate)*, a friendly local for many

Spaniards and Germans who live there. The bars and restaurants situated in Morro's two narrow main streets in the pedestrian zone are not geared to tourists. Creating an authentic atmosphere while also appealing to non-Spanish guests is something *Cantina de Mia (closed Sun. | C/ Carmen 9 | Budget)* does well. This friendly restaurant serves Canarian tapas, Italian pizza and pasta as well as hamburgers and is open for breakfast (from 8am onwards).

Among the many cafes and ice-cream parlours, the three worth mentioning are the popular *California (Av. Saladar/at the taxi stand Casa Atlántica)* for ice, crêpes, juices, cocktails, *Eisdealer (30 m/98 ft further west)* and the coffee shop selling ice cream *Magdalena (Av. Saladar 22d | on the hill near the petrol station).*

INSIDER TIP CORONADO

The cuisine on offer here is even more upmarket now and the menu stands out with its delicious combinations that blend Canarian, Mediterranean and Asian influences. The majority of the ingredients are sourced locally from the island – and you can certainly taste freshness. Reasonable prices and good portions. By the way, the *Coronado* also offers beautiful accomodation! *Thu–Tue, evenings only | next to the Riu Palace Jandía | tel. 9 28 54 11 74 | www.restaurantecoronado.com | Moderate–Expensive*

PICCOLA ITALIA

This restaurant has its own classic stone oven and serves the most delicious wood-fired pizzas in town. *Daily | C/ del Carmen 39 | tel. 9 28 54 12 58 | Budget*

STETSON

Those dining in this popular restaurant (which is situated in the rather ugly CC Cosmo) should rather focus on the food:

delicious steaks and other meat dishes, but also good fish, and wonderful creations for starters and desserts, everything lovingly prepared. Unfortunately nothing can hide the hideous interior design. *Only Tue–Sun evenings | CC Cosmo, upper floor | tel. 6 26 14 09 58 | www.gourmet-stetson.com | Expensive*

SHOPPING

The main road has a good selection of diverse shops and there are some bargains to be had shopping in Morro Jable. Approaching from Jandía you will reach the large supermarket *Padilla* on the right of the street going to the valley (before the turn to the left). Don't forget that Thursday is market day on the main road at the open space next to CC Cosmo.

MATTFISCH

Something new for a change: The chef Matthias Gramann prepares *jamón del mar* – ham made of fish. This dry-cured and pickled fish even tastes of ham but also melts in the mouth. His next brainwave is to start selling fish-filled rolls, surely a perfect snack. *C/ Mascona 32/ im Mercado Municipal (innen ganz links)*

SPORTS & ACTIVITIES

ACTIVITIES IN THE HARBOUR

There are quite a few to choose from and many of them are under one roof at *Excursiones Mar y Tierra (tel. 9 28 54 17 71 | www.excursionesmarytierra.com)* whose station is on a pontoon in the harbour: jet ski, banana boats, speed boats, waterskis, wakeboarding and deep sea fishing. The almost two hour long jet ski ride to the western cape is popular. For sport fishing you can also take the *Yellowfin (tel. 6 76 26 34 39)* out. Sail boats mean enjoyable trips (without engine noise). The catamarans are especially spacious. Apart from the *Magic* and the *Santa María*, more catamarans are moored in the harbour and can be booked with the tour guide at the hotel. Or do you prefer a more active pastime? Then why not set sail on "Maxi", a traditional monohull yacht. When the wind causes the boat to heel, or lean on its side, this gives even the laziest sun worshipper an adrenalin kick. The "Maxi" is not always harboured in the port because it undertakes longer sailing trips *(tel. 6 47 45 41 12 | www.maxisailing.es)*.

The two-mast *Pedra Sartaña,* built in 1940, takes to sea on Tuesdays to Saturdays at 9:30am and 2:30pm (in the winter 10:30am only) for the popular pirate tours *(tel. 6 70 74 51 91 | www.excursiones-barco-fuerteventura.com)* – great fun especially for kids. Take a first-row seat in the "Odyssee 3" glass-bottom catamaran to watch an underwater cinematic show. But that's not all: the boat will stop along the way for you to swim, dive or even snorkel in the turquoise waters. The boat also has a slide into the water for kids (and adults) *(tel. 6 16 43 71 84)*. All the harbour operators provide transfer from/ to your hotel.

BICYCLES
Volcano Bikes (station at the Club Aldiana | tel. 6 39 73 87 43 | www.volcano-bike.com) hires out bicycles and organises tours. Four-wheel pedal bikes can be rented at the wooden shed *Tourist Info Center* at the western end of the salt marsh.

FISH FOOT MASSAGE ●
Don't worry the fish in the water are not piranhas! They are helpful little sea creatures which nibble away at dry skin on your feet and legs – a delightfully relaxing treatment in the *Fish Spa (CC Cosmo, basement)*.

GOLF
The deserted 18-hole site has been restored to life: *Jandía Golf (par 71 | Barranco Vinamar | tel. 9 28 87 19 79 | www.jandiagolf.com)*.

MOTORBIKE, TRIKE & QUAD BIKE TRIPS
Trips through the area on dirt bikes and quads are offered by *Sahara Sports (tel. 6 69 79 71 62 | www.enduro-guru.com)*. INSIDER TIP Trike tours can be undertaken at *Xtreme (Av. del Saladar | at the CC Cosmo | tel. 9 28 87 56 30 | www.fuerte-trike.com)*. If you prefer an exciting offroad adventure, you can also book great buggy and quad tours there *(www.xtreme-car-rental.com)*. Scooters and quads are available at *Montes Quads (C/ Estrella del Mar | at the CC Faro | tel. 9 28 16 66 70)*.

SAILING & SURFING

The main providers for catamaran sailing, SUP and windsurfing in the area are the water sports centre on the beach side of the *Robinson Club (tel. 9 28 16 95 39)*.

BEACHES & SWIMMING

Even during high season, the almost 50 m/164 ft wide fine golden sand Jandía Playa *(Playa de Matorral)* beach is never crowded but renting two loungers and

Catamarans are moored at the beach in Morro Jable waiting for adventurous sailors

Below the *Club Aldiana, Surfers Island (tel. 9 28 16 63 49)* not only offers windsurfing, SUP and ●catamaran sailing but also surfing (rental and courses).

SEGWAYS & ELECTRIC SCOOTERS

Get on a pair of electric wheels on a guided tour at *Senda Ventura (east of the town between Iberostar and Club Aldiana | tel. 6 38 67 95 04 | www.segway-fuerteventura.de/en.* A more individual and ecological means of travel is by electric scooter for hire at *TabataRent (tel. 6 58 86 76 57)* at the tennis centre near *Labranda World.*

an umbrella will cost you a rather hefty 13.50 euros per day. Nude bathing close to the town is frowned upon.

SCUBA DIVING

The *Felix diving centre (to the west next to CC Faro off the main road | tel. 6 22 19 66 10 | www.fuerteventurabuceo. com)* is now managed by Niko who will take you by boat to the best diving spots around the island.

TENNIS

The better hotels offer artificial grass and clay courts. Lessons at *Matchpoint Sports*

MORRO JABLE/JANDÍA PLAYA

(tel. 9 28 54 43 07 | www.matchpoint-world.com).

ENTERTAINMENT

The best way to kick off your evening is with a sundowner on the rooftop garden of ● *El Navegante* down in Morro Jable: Its "2-4-1" (two for one) happy hour offers two drinks for the price of one. The "Sailor" is the favourite open-air lounge

the owner who takes out his own guitar. *California (at the taxi stand Casa Atlántica)* also attracts guests with its well-mixed cocktails (including non-alcoholic ones) and gin-based long drinks. In CC Palm Garden, *Bar Oasis* is the biggest crowd-puller with the occasional live band and great cocktails. Fridays and Saturdays are club night, starting in *Skipper (in CC Faro/first floor, at Hotel Faro)* with a round of pool and continuing on

No matter where you stay – there is always a sea view

bar for insiders. The town's INSIDER TIP live music scene is worth checking out. Although the *Navegante* bar has suffered from noise protection laws, there are two alternative music venues nearby: *El Callao* on the other side of the barranco regularly gives musicians a platform to play on their terrace – as well as cheap tapas to hungry guests. Next door to the *Navegante,* the traditional *San Borondón* is a meeting point for Spanish locals and tourists alike, who come to see the guitar-playing duo Jorge & José, watch the occasional karaoke singer or

after midnight to the *Guru* club *(CC Cosmo, first floor).*

WHERE TO STAY

In Jandía Playa accommodation options are mainly in large hotel complexes. If you prefer accommodation with a more personal atmosphere, you should go to Morro Jable.

ATALAYA DE JANDÍA

This exquisite complex seems to be suspended above the sea and is right in the front of the rocks in the west of Morro Jable, above the church. The 20 spacious apartments have their own balconies and the complex also has a small swimming pool. *C/ Los Guanches 46 | tel. 9 28 54 02 27 | www.esmeraldaresorts. com | Expensive*

CASA ALBERTO

12 small apartments or studios with sea views that are simply but adequately equipped. Fantastic roof terraces! *Av. del Faro 4 | Morro Jable | tel. 9 28 1667 00 | www.casa-alberto-apartamentos.com | Budget*

CASABLANCA

Small, leafy complex run by Germans, with 12 well-equipped apartments or studios (with sea view). Small swimming pool in the shape of Fuerteventura! *Av. del Faro 8 | on the slope above Morro Jable | tel. 9 28 54 17 44 | www.apartamentos-casablanca.com | Moderate*

FARO JANDÍA

A vibrant-looking hotel. Because of its central location it's a good choice for those who like to do things outside of the hotel. The 214 rooms (all with own balcony, many with sea views) are air-conditioned. The hotel has a swimming pool,

fitness room, tennis courts and mini golf. The large well-run spa area *Las Caricias del Faro (tel. 9 28 16 70 74)* has a swimming pool, sauna, Turkish bath, massages and beauty treatments. You do not have to be a guest of the hotel to use the spa. *Av. del Saladar | lighthouse hill | tel. 9 28 54 50 35 | www.murhoteles.com | Expensive*

OCCIDENTAL JANDÍA PLAYA/ OCCIDENTAL JANDÍA MAR

This double hotel complex is situated on the large roundabout above the town and claims to be the town's cheapest four-star resort. The more expensive lower part *Jandía Playa (634 rooms)* is closer to the beach and offers the better sea views; this also includes an adult-only premium zone *(another 80 rooms)* offering all-inclusive accommodation. In contrast, the *Jandía Mar (485 rooms)* in the upper part is intended for families with children. Some of these rooms have a sliding door to convert them into small family suites. The underground exit from Jandía Playa takes you into the CC Ventura with a supermarket and two bars; from there, a pedestrian tunnel leads to the beach. *Jandía Playa: tel. 9 28 54 60 00, Jandía Mar: tel. 9 28 54 65 00, both: www. barcelo.com | Expensive*

ALTERNATIVE PLACE NAMES

Something as official as a place name should be constant, one would think. This is not the case on Fuerteventura. Instead of Morro Jable one can also say Morro del Jable, you can say Vega de Río de las Palmas or Vega de Río Palma. The holiday resort in the bay Caleta de Fustes completely con-

fuses with its six different names: for instance Costa Caleta, Playa de Castillo, Castillo de Fuste or El Castillo... Many places have an article in front of the name like La Antigua or La Oliva, but it is often simply omitted. There are no set rules as to which one should be used when.

OCEAN WORLD

The hotel for scuba divers! *Ocean World* is primarily a diving centre with three different bases dotted around the island. It also offers accommodation in its 17-room hotel with a small pool and decent restaurant. There is also a bike station to keep divers fit when on shore *(schnixx-bike.com)*. *C/ Flamenco 2 | in the valley next to Labranda World | tel. 9 28 54 03 24 | www.oceanworld-hotels. com | Moderate*

ROBINSON CLUB JANDÍA PLAYA

The palm-lined resort with swimming pool – and everything else that you might expect from a club in this price range – is the only one situated in the flat foreshore on the beach. In 2010 they celebrated their 40th anniversary – as the oldest of all Robinson Clubs. The club is great for young couples and singles – the club in Esquinzo is better suited to families. The 350 rooms are divided between the air-conditioned hotel high-rise and the two-storied buildings in the large garden. Sporting activities include tennis, scuba diving and windsurfing. In 2018, the club will close for a year for a general overhaul. *Jandía Playa on the main road | tel. 9 28 16 91 00 | www.robinson.com | Expensive (full board)*

OFICINA DE TURISMO

Mon–Fri 8am–3pm | in the basement of the CC Cosmo | tel. 9 28 54 07 76

WHERE TO GO

PICO DE LA ZARZA ★ ☼
(132 C5) *(ᗰ C2)*

Before enjoying yourself, you have to endure a bit of torture: it's uphill for three hours, and what is more, you'll also have to get up early. Your destination:The summit of Pico de la Zarza, at 807 m/2647.6 ft the highest summit on the island, also known as *Pico de Jandía* – and only accessible by foot. The hike as such is not very difficult. Normal walking shoes should do – flip-flops are definitely not an option. Once you have found the entrance point, you cannot get lost as the path has been walked many times so it is easy to identify. When the summit is not surrounded by trade wind clouds, the view from the top is quite overwhelming. Increase your chances of a clear view by hiking up in the morning rather than in the afternoon.

The starting point is at the large roundabout at the Jandía Playa village entrance, where the country road and the salt marsh meet. Take the wide road past *CC Ventura* and the hotel *Occidental Jandía Playa*. Just behind the hotel, you turn left and after about 600 m/1970 ft turn right (uphill) into a cul-de-sac from which 200 m/ 656 ft further to the right a track slips out. Now you only need to follow the track. At about 700 m/2,300 ft you will reach the fence that surrounds the summit area in order to keep out hungry goats. At this height the trade wind clouds provide enough precipitation so that protected plants thrive between the rocks. In order to protect these plants for the future, please ensure that you close the gate behind you. From here a narrow, winding path leads steeply up to the ridge, follow the ridge to the right to reach the summit.

Your hike should take about five hours under normal conditions and walking at a moderate pace. You should bear in mind that there is no food available along the way and of course you should take enough water along. At the top you will have to reckon with strong winds and

A South American feel: lonely coastal landscape near Cofete

you should take something warm along to wear. Just as important is good sun protection (hat and sunscreen), because there is no shade.

WESTERN CAPE AND COFETE ★ ●

The extreme western tip of the island, the *Punta de Jandía,* is often falsely referred to as the south cape, when Morro Jable is clearly more southern. The trip to Punta de Jandía, over a dusty bumpy road is still quite a bit of an adventure – an off-road vehicle is the best option. There are two destinations worth visiting here. There is the little fishing village *Puerto de la Cruz* (132 A6) *(𝄞 A3)* which has three pubs that all serve fresh seafood. There is an exhibition in the nearby lighthouse, which runs on solar energy, giving more information about local marine life *(Tue–Sun 10:30am–5:30pm)*. On a clear day you can see Gran Canaria from here.

Cofete (132 C5) *(𝄞 C2),* the most remote town on the island, consists of a few houses and shacks that use their own generators for electricity and there is no running water. The few remaining inhabitants live off goat farming and the tourists that visit the *Bar Cofete (Moderate)* for its fish soup. The main attraction however, is the *Villa Winter* surrounded as it is in a shroud of mystery. More about this as well as the stretch in between in the chapter "Discovery Tours", tour no. 4.

There is also the option to walk to Cofete on one of the INSIDERTIP old royal roads *(camino reales)*. Drive 3.2 km/1.9 miles from the harbour to *Gran Valle*, where you can walk from the car park (signposted: Red de Caminos de Pájara). Keep going straight up the valley. The track has been revamped and you cannot get lost. There and back should take about four hours, so take some snacks and water along. 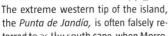 There is a wonderful view from the mountain saddle.

DISCOVERY TOURS

1

FUERTEVENTURA AT A GLANCE

START: **1** Morro Jable/Jandía Playa **END:** **14** Corralejo	**9 hours** Driving time (without stops) approx. 3 hours
Distance: ➡ **175 km/109 miles**	

COSTS: 55 euros for hire car (compact car) and petrol, approx.
50 euros per person for admission costs, lunch and dinner
WHAT TO PACK: sun protection, swimwear

IMPORTANT TIPS: Return to Morro Jable is 120 km/75 miles (approx.
1 ¾ hour). Do not take this tour on Sundays, Mondays or Bank Holidays
to ensure that all the shops and restaurants are open yet not too busy.
Set off at 9am at the latest in summer and even earlier in winter.

Would you like to explore the places that are unique to this island? Then the Discovery Tours are just the thing for you – they include terrific tips for stops worth making, breathtaking places to visit, selected restaurants and fun activities. It's even easier with the Touring App: download the tour with map and route to your smartphone using the QR Code on pages 2/3 or from the website address in the footer below – and you'll never get lost again even when you're offline.

TOURING
APP

→ p. 2/3

Experience the diversity Fuerteventura has to offer on this tour that takes you right across the island: from Morro Jable/Jandía Playa in the south to Corralejo in the north. Take in the mountain landscape, beaches, fantastic views and a meal in the nicest restaurant on the island.

09:00am The tour starts in the south of the island at ❶ **Morro Jable/Jandía Playa** → p. 81. First head to the spectacular lagoon in front of Playa Barca → p. 78. The best view over the lagoon can be had from a ❷ **viewpoint near Risco del Paso** to the south of Playa Barca; to

❶ Morro Jable/
Jandía Playa

17 km/10.6 mi

❷ viewpoint near Risco del Paso

Fuerteventura

3 Costa Calma

9 km/5.6 mi

4 La Pared

8 km/5 mi

5 Mirador Sicasumbre

12 km/7.5 mi

get there, **exit the motorway (700 m/2,300 ft from the exit El Salmo). Then drive back to the FV2 main road,** following it to Costa Calma. On the way, you will be dazzled by the whiteness of the sand on both sides of the road: The island's trade winds transport it cross country from the north-eastern coast of the peninsula down to the south. **Once you have passed through ❸ Costa Calma → p. 71 with its luscious green palm trees, turn left towards La Pared, taking a north-western route along the Istmo de la Pared.** On reaching ❹ La Pared → p. 77 the landscape changes from sandy white to a red clay-grey. At the top of the pass below the Tablada mountain, stop the car at ❺ **Mirador Sicasumbre** to take the signposted path up the hill. The south westerly view takes in the coastline while the desolate mountain landscape with its herds of goats stretches to the north and east.

11:00am Shortly before arriving in Pájara, take a detour to the left to ⑥ **Ajuy** → **p. 67**. This former fishing village with its dark sandy beach is the starting point for a gentle stroll to the nearby ancient lime kilns and "pirate caves". With its jagged cliffs and crashing waves, this offers you a different picture of Fuerteventura away from its tourist sandy beaches. Stop in ⑦ **Pájara** → **p. 66** to visit its church with its Aztec-inspired main entrance and while there take your first break for the day in **La Fonda** (*Budget*) opposite the church. Now comes the most adventurous part of the tour **along a narrow road winding uphill to the mountain's massif.** When you reach the top, stop to take in the views over what was once a reservoir and now covers the top of the Barranco de las Penitas → **p. 60** which cuts into the valley below. Now go downhill to ⑧ **Vega de Río de las Palmas**. The small chapel is the island's most popular destination for pilgrims. Well-hidden inland, set into the deep valley is the small town of ⑨ **Betancuria** → **p. 58**, the island's most historical setting. Two hours can be enjoyably spent here visiting the church as well as the multimedia show in **Casa Santa María**, where you can also enjoy a light meal in possibly the island's nicest restaurant and buy cactus jams and handicrafts.

04:00pm Follow the tight bends up the road to the ⑩ **Mirador Morro Velosa** → **p. 59** with its amazing panoramic view over the north of the island. **Now continue to Antigua, there take a right onto the FV 20 out of the town heading towards La Corte and the airport** (*Aeropuerto*). The road takes you past fields of aloe vera. Take a left turn signposted to the island's capital/airport where after a few kilometres you will soon reach ⑪ **Salinas del Carmen** → **p. 64**, the salt lakes with a salt museum. Here you'll need at least half an hour. **Drive past the golfing ranges of Caleta de Fustes and the airport until you reach the island's capital** ⑫ **Puerto del Rosario** → **p. 48**. **Take a right at the first roundabout, along the seashore and harbour, stopping after just 900 m/2,950 ft.** At the tourist information, located at the next major roundabout, you can pick up the leaflet "Puerto on foot", a guide to the city's many sculptures. Grab a refreshing ice cream at the **Kiss** (*Av. 1° del Mayo*) ice-cream parlour. The last part of the

19 km/12 mi

⑥ Ajuy

10.5 km/6.5 mi

⑦ Pájara

11 km/7 mi

⑧ Vega de Río de las Palmas

6 km/3.7 mi

⑨ Betancuria

3 km/1.9 mi

⑩ Mirador Morro Velosa

31 km/19 mi

⑪ Salinas del Carmen

16 km/10 mi

⑫ Puerto del Rosario

26 km/16 mi

⑬ shifting sand dunes of El Jable 🏖

5 km/3 mi

⑭ Corralejo 🍴

journey to Corralejo continues to the volcanic landscape in the island's north. **You'll reach this region's main attraction from the south – or via Corralejo as soon as the new road is finished:** the white **⑬ shifting sand dunes of El Jable** → p. 33. Plans were to close the road through the dunes back in 2012 however the construction of the new road has been continually delayed. To round off your tour, enjoy dinner and the sea view in **⑭ Corralejo** → p. 32 at **El Anzuelo** before heading home.

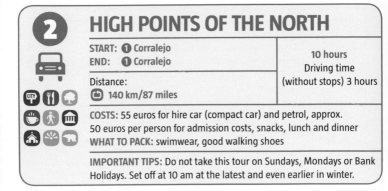

② HIGH POINTS OF THE NORTH

START: ❶ Corralejo	10 hours
END: ❶ Corralejo	Driving time (without stops) 3 hours
Distance: 🚗 140 km/87 miles	

COSTS: 55 euros for hire car (compact car) and petrol, approx. 50 euros per person for admission costs, snacks, lunch and dinner
WHAT TO PACK: swimwear, good walking shoes

IMPORTANT TIPS: Do not take this tour on Sundays, Mondays or Bank Holidays. Set off at 10 am at the latest and even earlier in winter.

This round trip around the north takes you through the island's capital, along the west coast's steep cliffs and to the sacred mountain Tindaya. An open-air museum provides an interesting insight into how the island's native inhabitants once lived.

❶ Corralejo

30.5 km/19 mi

❷ Puerto del Rosario 🏙☕

28.5 km/17.7 mi

`10:00am` Start in **❶ Corralejo** → p. 32 and head for your first destination at **❷ Puerto del Rosario** → p. 48, or "Port of the Rosary". A normal weekday morning is the perfect time to take a stroll around the island's capital. **Leave the FV-1 at the first exit and follow the signs to "Puerto".** When you reach the harbour promenade, you will see the tourist information's pavilion on the roundabout with the large fountain decorated with sculptures. Here you can grab a map of the city. After wandering around the city, take brunch at **El Perenquén,** a pleasant spot with a view over the harbour.

`12:00pm` Head out of the city on the FV-20 towards Antigua. After leaving Casillas del Angel, take a right in the direction of Betancuria and at the next roundabout, take another right to Oliva. From the FV-207

on which you're now driving, your route soon takes a
left turn onto the access road FV-221 heading to Par-
celas and Molinos. When you reach ❸ INSIDER TIP ▶ Puertito de los Molinos ("small mill harbour") at the end
of this road, you'll catch a glimpse of the island's wild
west coast. This is the smallest fishing village on the island and looks as if it could belong to another century. Affluent city dwellers have their weekend residenc-
es here. A footbridge at the end of the road leads you
over a Barranco filled with water all year round; a shrine
with mother and child stands on a square in the village
– this naïvely decorated folk art sculpture is from the
fishermen in honour of their patron saint. The bar-res-

❸ Puertito de los Moli-
nos 🏠 🍴 🏃 🌊 🌳

13.5 km/8.4 mi

Canarian home decor at the
Ecomuseo La Alcogida

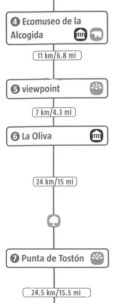

4 Ecomuseo de la
Alcogida

11 km/6.8 mi

5 viewpoint

7 km/4.3 mi

6 La Oliva

24 km/15 mi

7 Punta de Tostón

24.5 km/15.5 mi

taurant **Casa Pon** *(Budget)* offers good refreshments and snacks as well as a splendid sea view terrace. From the small car park at the entrance to the village or along the beach (which unfortunately is not really suited for bathing), you will reach a staircase path heading south to a viewpoint on the cliffs: an amazing point to witness the waves crashing onto the barren westerly coastline.

02:00pm Head back to the FV-207, turn left to Tefia and after 1.25 km/0.8 miles you'll soon reach the 4 **Ecomuseo de la Alcogida** → p. 108. The open-air museum's car park and visitor's centre are on the left-hand side. Plan 90 minutes for the tour around the museum. **Then head further north through the scattered settlement of Tefía. Take a left onto the FV-10** where you'll soon spot the Montaña Quemada → p. 47 with its life-like image of the poet Miguel de Unamuno. Soon after you'll reach Tindaya. The village is named after the red mountain to the north, the Montaña de Tindaya → p. 47. Rather than climbing it (which is not permitted anyway), head right up the winding road towards Vallebrón. The 5 **viewpoint** above the pass offers a splendid panoramic view with the sacred mountain of the native Canarians in the distance.

04:30pm Your next station is 6 **La Oliva** → p. 45. There is plenty to see here, in particular the magnificent fortress-style **Casa de los Coroneles**, the **church**, the art gallery **Centro de Arte Canario** and the grain museum **Casa de la Cilla. On the FV-10 to Cotillo take a small detour over Lajares** → **p. 44.** Although the embroidery school has probably closed by now, make a point of **taking the old road to Cotillo from the roundabout** through old fields covered in lava stone and enclosed with lava stone walls – an unusual cultural landscape with a strange appeal.

07:00pm Try to catch the sunset at the 7 **Punta de Tostón** → p. 45, the most north-westerly point of the island. **To get there, take a right through Cotillo** → p. 42. It doesn't matter if you arrive early: You can also enjoy the evening sunset from the harbour's fortress tower or even better at one of the sea-view restaurants. After a good meal, **head back to ❶ Corralejo via Lajares**.

❶ Corralejo

❸ NATIVE CANARIANS AND MAJOREROS

START: ❶ Pájara	7 ½ hours
END: ❼ Pozo Negro	Driving time (without stops) 1½ hr, hike approx. 1½ hr
Distance: easy	
⊝ 50 km/31 mi ▪▪▮ Height: 150 m/492 ft	

COSTS: 45 euros for hire car and petrol, approx. 25 euros per person for admission costs, snacks, lunch

WHAT TO PACK: hiking shoes, sun protection, water

IMPORTANT TIPS: Do not take the tour on Sundays or Bank Holidays.

This tour takes you to the heart of the island into the mountains where you can discover how the island's native Canarians and so-called Majoreros once lived.

09:00am Once you have reached ❶ Pájara → p. 65 either from the south via La Pared or otherwise Tuineje, you'll have your first encounter with the island's culture. The **church** is a must-see here. Then take a coffee break in the country hotel **Casa Isaítas** (from the crossroads at the church, go 100 m/328 ft in the direction of Betancuria and it is on the left-hand side), since this is a traditional Canarian estate renovated to its original style.

❶ Pájara

8.5 km/5.3 mi

10:30am Now the tour takes you inland into the mountains. The next stop is ❷ Risco de las Peñas, a 426 m/1,400 ft high viewpoint which looks down onto a dried-up reservoir, your next port of call (on foot). In the distance, you can spot a tiny white cube, the chapel of Ermita de la Peña. The journey continues downhill to Vega de Río de las Palmas → p. 59. When you reach the bottom, **turn left (signposted: "Vega de Río Palma") and follow this small road for another 1.1 km.** The next stage of this trip is to be taken on foot through the ❸ Barranco de las Peñitas → p. 60, as described on page 60, until you reach the **Casa de la Naturaleza** where you've now deserved a bite to eat. Situated 120 m/394 ft in front of the bridge, this authentically renovated estate has been successfully converted into a museum and restaurant where

❷ Risco de las Peñas

4 km/2.5 mi

❸ Barranco de las Peñitas

9.5 km/6 mi

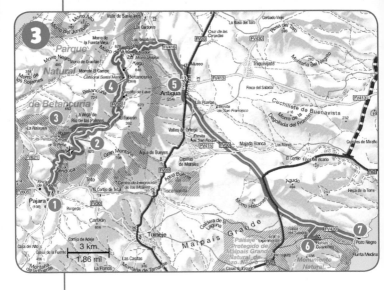

you can relax and soak in its splendid gardens, pond and traditional design.

02:00pm Head back to the main road and take a left to ❹ **Betancuria** → p. 58. Once the island's capital, this town is now the most popular inland destination with its monastery ruins, church, museums and an abundance of arts and crafts. Don't miss out on the INSIDER TIP multi media show in the **Casa Santa María** as well as its exhibition and splendid garden! A visit to the compact **Archaeological Museum** would also be an appropriate stop on this cultural tour.

04:00pm After a further 3 km/1.9 miles uphill, you will be welcomed by the colossal tribesmen statues of Guize and Ayose – as well as a fantastic panoramic view over the north of the island. The road now heads down to ❺ **Antigua** → p. 54. **Take a left at the church in Antigua and then another left onto the FV-20.** Head north and after a few hundred metres you can visit the **cheese museum** with the old mill as its dominating feature.

Now head back home through Antigua and take a left onto the FV-50 airport-bound *(Aeropuerto)*. Once you have left the suburb of La Corte, you'll drive past aloe

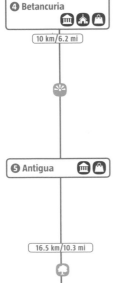

❹ Betancuria

10 km/6.2 mi

❺ Antigua

16.5 km/10.3 mi

Fascinating mountains: viewpoint near Antigua

vera fields and come to the FV-2. Take a right here and then exit this road almost immediately to head for Pozo Negro. After 3 km/1.9 miles, turn right to the native Canarian ruins of ⑥ Atalayita → p. 56, the only point on the island that offers a glimpse of how the aboriginal inhabitants lived on the island in precolonial times. The tour ends with a well-earned meal taken on a sea-view terrace of one of the fish restaurants in ⑦ Pozo Negro!

⑥ Atalayita

4.5 km/2.8 mi

⑦ Pozo Negro

④ TO THE WESTERN CAPE AND VILLA WINTER

START: ❶ Morro Jable/Jandía Playa	6 ½ hours
END: ❶ Morro Jable/Jandía Playa	Driving time (without stops)
Distance: 65 km/40 miles	3 hours

COSTS: 125 euros for hire car (jeep) and petrol plus approx. 15 euros per person for lunch
WHAT TO PACK: water to drink and a packed lunch

IMPORTANT TIPS: As some of the dirt roads on this tour require an off-road vehicle, it is essential that you hire a jeep. If you make the mistake of taking a normal hire car, you will be in breach of the hire contract and will not be covered by your insurance.

Driving along the western tip of the Jandía peninsula is an adventure: rugged, desolate landscape and a wild coastline

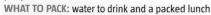

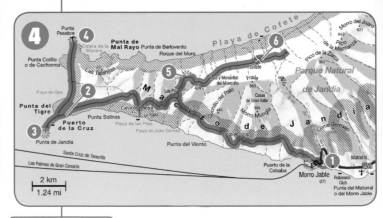

❶ Morro Jable/ Jandía Playa

20 km/12.5 mi

❷ Puerto de la Cruz ☕ 🌸

1.5 km/0.9 mi

❸ Punta de Jandía 🏛

5.5 km/3.4 mi

❹ Punta Pesebre 🌳

12.5 km/7.8 mi

❺ Roque del Moro 🌸

9 km/5.6 mi

10:00am **First take the bypass road around ❶ Morro Jable/Jandía Playa → p. 81. Shortly before you reach the port of Morro Jable, turn right onto the signposted track.** While the first section is still surfaced, the rest of the way is a bumpy dirt track with just one patch of tarmacked surface in-between. This 20 km dirt road follows the coastline, separated from the shore by a stretch of deserted land. Shortly before you reach the narrow peninsula of Punta de Jandía with its lighthouse jutting out into the sea, you'll arrive in the unassuming village of ❷ **Puerto de la Cruz** which is a good spot for a break and bite to eat at **El Caletón** (Budget–Moderate), even with sea view!

11:30am In Puerto de la Cruz, you'll have to leave the beaten track to visit two must-see attractions: The first is the lighthouse at the most south-westerly point of the island on the ❸ **Punta de Jandía** peninsula to the south of the village. Unfortunately the small museum in the lighthouse does not have regular opening times. **Back in Puerto de la Cruz opposite the Punta Jandía bar, a tarmacked pothole-filled road takes you north to the nearby ❹ Punta Pesebre.** This is the remotest part of island which can be reached by car. On the way, you'll pass by an old runway on your right which was never in use.

01:30pm **Now head back to Morro Jable until you reach a crossroads, taking a left onto a mountain pass to the northern coast and Cofete.** You will soon, at the ❺ **Roque del Moro,** reach the INSIDER TIP most spectacular viewing platform on the island's southern coast. If you're driving with the windows open, take care that the wind does not blow anything out of the car or your hat off! The light sandy beach of Playa de Cofete stretches out below you with the "small island" of El Islote at its easterly point. Beyond, you can see the vast beach of Playa de Barlovento, and on a clear day the north-easterly view extends all the way to the mountains at Pájara. From the beaches, the slopes stretch upwards to the 807 m/ 2,648 ft high Pico de Jandía (also known as Pico de la Zarza), the island's highest peak. Off this beaten track, you'll notice the towering *euphorbieae*, the long candelabra-shaped flowering plants that resemble cacti.

02:30pm The next stop is ❻ **Cofete** → p. 89. Before reaching this seemingly forgotten settlement, you'll notice a two-storey building with a round tower standing alone on the hillside in front of you: This is the legendary **Villa Winter**, **only to be reached by jeep or on foot.** As legend has it, the German engineer Gustav Winter (1893–1971), who leased the whole of the peninsula Jandía in 1937, used it as a submarine base for the German navy. By studying the archives and interviewing witnesses around at the time, two German residents on the island proved that there is in fact little evidence to support this legend just as the many other rumours circulating about this old villa. The building was never entirely finished and was never inhabited, however under Franco, the entire peninsula belonged to "Don Gustavos", as he was commonly known on the island. Winter ruled over his enormous hacienda like a lord. It was then divided into four parts and sold by 1964. Today the villa is home to goatherds. Although there are no regular visits organised, a little cash in hand can usually open the villa's doors. Its transformation into a museum has been decided.

Resist the temptation to carry on along the endless sandy beaches; it is strictly forbidden to drive cross-country in this nature reserve and if caught, you will be forced to pay a hefty fine. **Instead, take the route back to** ❶ **Morro Jable/Jandía Playa.**

Shrouded in mystery: Villa Winter near Cofete

❻ Cofete

14 km/8.7 mi

❶ Morro Jable/ Jandía Playa

SPORTS & ACTIVITIES

Whether you like swimming, strolling along beaches or lying on warm sand – Fuerteventura offers all-inclusive sport and relaxation for everyone. If this is not enough, the island offers even more, especially for those wanting to try out water sports. The five-star hotels are the best addresses for massages and spas; or why not visit the Thalasso Spa in Caleta de Fustes for a foot-tingling fish massage!

Addresses of sports companies not listed below can be found under the Sports & Activities sections for the individual towns. The expression "in all the large holiday resorts" refers to: Corralejo, Caleta de Fustes, Costa Calma/La Pared and Jandía Playa/Morro Jable.

BICYCLES & MOTORBIKES

INSIDER TIP Cycling has become a very popular sport and there are rentals available at all the large holiday resorts as well as Las Playitas. They often also have organised mountain bike trips in varying degrees of difficulty, most of them are not too demanding: you can be motor powered uphill and then freewheel downhill. Racing cyclists fly out to the island to train in the winter months. If you prefer to experience the island under your own steam you should avoid the main roads where possible. A bicycle network is currently under construction. Helmets are compulsory outside built-up areas and the alcohol limit also applies to cyclists. Motorcycle trips with dirt bikes

An island for anyone wanting to enjoy sporting activities in, under, or on the water

or quad bikes are also available in all the large holiday resorts.

FISHING

Motor boat trips for off-coast fishing or deep sea fishing depart from Corralejo and Morro Jable but can be booked from elsewhere with transfer from/to your hotel. The operators provide the equipment and offer discounts to non-fishing passengers.

GOLF

Golf took off on the island in 2002 when the 18-hole course at Caleta de Fustes was opened *(par 70, with driving range, putting green, etc. | tel. 9 28 16 00 34)*. Today there are three additional 18-hole courses: *Salinas de Antigua* (next to the first one), *Jandía Golf* near Jandía Playa and *Las Playitas*, the latter is part of the sports centre *Playitas Grand Resort*. There is also the *golf academy (tel.*

9 28 54 91 03) in La Pared, where you can learn how to play golf with Irish pro Ken Ellis. There is a six-hole course and a driving range. Holiday clubs and some hotels also offer driving ranges and putting greens.

HIKING

For anyone who is interested in nature and the traditional lifestyle of the islanders, the island interior has some interesting surprises. The hike through the Barranco de las Peñitas is thoroughly explained in Vega de Río de las Palmas, so you can easily manage it on your own. It gets really exciting when you take a ★● *guided hike* with an English speaking guide. They will have fascinating insights about the local flora, fauna, history and geography. *Bookings at the travel agents in the hotels*

HORSERIDING

The German-run stable *Rancho Barranca de los Caballos* (see p. 78) near La Pared offers INSIDER TIP rides out to the rugged west coast – giving you a true feeling of Fuerteventura adventure and freedom. In the north, the *Granja Tara* stables (see p. 43) is similar, while at Caleta de Fustes, you should contact *Crines del Viento (northern town exit in Triquivijate | tel. 6 78 21 31 08 | www. crinesdelviento.com).*

SAILING

You can learn to sail on catamarans at the *Club Aldiana* at Jandía Playa, the *Robinson Clubs* of Esquinzo and Jandía Playa, in Tarajalejo and in Las Playitas. If you just want to relax on a yacht it can be arranged in Corralejo, Morro Jable/Jandía Playa as well as Caleta de Fustes. Most tours include drinks and lunch on board as well as stops for swimming and snorkelling. For skippers: there are yacht marinas in Caleta de Fustes, Corralejo, Gran Tarajal, Morro Jable and Puerto del Rosario.

SCUBA DIVING

★ *Scuba diving* on Fuerteventura is a lot of fun and dive sites like the El Río straits at Corralejo, the moray eel reef in front of Jandía Playa and various other spots are all popular. The island's lava formations and diverse marine treasures make it one of the best diving areas in the Canaries. Scuba diving schools are based in all the large holiday resorts as well as Las Playitas. To learn to dive you first need a medical certificate but there are a number of local doctors who provide this service. Ask at the diving schools.

TENNIS

Good hotels and clubs have artificial grass and clay courts with wind protection but some may only have concrete courts or insufficient protection against the wind. Lessons are offered in various hotels in the south by *Matchpoint Sports (tel. 9 28 54 43 07 | www.matchpoint-world.com).*

WATERSKI, JET SKI & BANANA BOATS

The two-seater jet skis need no introduction and at about 70 euros for 30 minutes, they can be both an expensive and a noisy ride. To get the best jet ski value for money try the companies in the harbour at Morro Jable. Companies that offer jet skis often also rent out banana boats (yellow structures on

Just take the plunge – off Fuerteventura, that's a fruitful endeavour

which several people can sit and which are then towed along behind a motor boat at high speed). There are jet ski companies in all the large holiday resorts. Some of them also offer waterskiing

WINDSURFING & SURFING

⭐ *Windsurfing* is the main water sport on the island. The wind and water conditions are ideal all year with the strongest wind blowing during the summer. The lowest wind speeds – with occasional lulls – are from November to January. Whether you're a beginner, advanced or an ace there will be just the right spot for you on Fuerteventura. The most important spots are the Playas de Sotavento on the Jandía peninsula, the area around Corralejo and – only for the experts – the beaches in El Cotillo. Surf schools and equipment rentals can be found in all the large holiday resorts.

INSIDER TIP Kitesurfing is also a very trendy sport and popular spots are Corralejo's dune beach as well as Playa Barca in the south. Kitesurfers use a surfboard combined with a large kite that functions as a sail, the board is powered by the wind. Nearly all windsurf stations also offer stand-up paddling (SUP). Surf sites for normal surfboarders are along the west coast and on the north coast. There are surf companies in Lajares (e.g. *Joyas Surf | tel. 6 65 03 50 66)* or in Costa Calma/La Pared *(Waveguru | tel. 6 19 80 44 47)*.

The innovative owner of *Otro Modo Surfschool (tel. 3 46 75 17 00 04 | www.otro-modo-surfschool.com)* came up with the wonderful idea of combining surfing with Spanish lessons. There are surf spots with accommodation in bungalows or apartments at Costa Calma and Morro Jable. So while your body takes a rest your brain can get busy with a conversation course. The language classes take place in small groups.

TRAVEL WITH KIDS

There are numerous possibilities for children of all ages to experience something fun and exciting on Fuerteventura. Most hotels, apartments and resort complexes are geared towards families and children and offer all kinds of entertainment. They cater across the range from affordable, self-catering apartments for the budget-conscious all the way up to the holiday clubs, where professional entertainers keep the children busy all (or almost all) of the time.

Experiencing the island's nature usually ranks right up at the top for children. In places like ● *Puertito de los Molinos*, where there are some good vantage points on the rocky west coast, the sea with its crashing waves and spray makes for a magnificent spectacle. The island's wonderful sandy beaches and the joy of swimming in the sea is a priceless – and free! – pleasure for every child. Having said that, a word of warning: it is best not to holiday on the island with pre-school kids during spring or summer when gusting winds often whip up the sand making a visit to the beach unsuitable for small children. This is also when the summer sun is at its harshest and not ideal for very small children.

The south of the island and Caleta de Fustes are both good areas for children as bathing is safe all year round. An accommodation option that is particularly child-friendly is the *Robinson Club Esquinzo* which offers something for children of all ages. In Caleta de Fustes the *Barceló Castillo Beach Resort* is the best choice. The accommodation is

The island has a lot to offer children – whether it is the beach, go-carting, camel riding, the zoo or the aquarium – they are bound to have fun

at ground level, they offer some good entertainment options and the complex is right on a beach that has calm shallow surf, that you can look out over. The apartment hotel *Playitas Grand Resort* in Las Playitas is also a good choice for families with children as they also have a Kids Sports Academy with an entertainment emphasis on sport. But of course many other hotels on the island offer suitable entertainment options – only the "adults only" places are of course out of the question.

Many scuba diving schools also offer *scuba diving courses for children* who already know how to swim. The companies that offer the courses are in Corralejo, Costa Calma and Morro Jable/Jandía Playa. Children can also expend some energy and jump on the *trampoline* in Corralejo *(Calle Carabela, at the CC Plaza off the main road)* and in the playground in the centre of Caleta de Fustes. *Mini golf* is offered at Corralejo (on the premises of Acua Park, east side, and in the Calle

Carabela) as well as several large hotels like the *Playitas Grand Resort,* the *Faro Jandia* in Jandía Playa (also for non-guests) or at the *Barceló Fuerteventura* in Caleta de Fustes.

THE WHOLE ISLAND

INSIDER TIP BOAT TRIPS

At Corralejo there are cruises on the motorised catamaran "Celia Cruz" which has underwater windows (127 E1) *(𝄞 G2)* offering views of the world under the sea *(20 euros, children 10 euros).* The same goes for the "Odyssee 3" from Morro Jable. During the cruise there is not much to see, but once the boat stops you can feed the fish and it is really quite beautiful.

From Caleta de Fustes (131 E3) *(𝄞 G8)* a semi-submarine offers the same option *(15 euros, children 5 euros).* In the *Oceanarium* you can also experience the fish and sea lions up close.

THE NORTH

ECOMUSEO DE LA ALCOGIDA ★ ●
(130 B1) *(𝄞 E6)*

The outdoor museum in Tefía is the largest on the island. It consists of seven restored farms where the rooms are furnished as they were one hundred years ago, showing what a household looked like. A cinema shows films with farmers and their wives baking bread and dyeing. On two of the farms they have also faithfully reproduced some workshops. Children enjoy the *Casa Señor Teodosio* the most as is has a *gofio* mill with a donkey turning the capstan wheel. There are also other animals to see. One house further along they sometimes demonstrate how bread is baked in a wood oven. A basket weaver at work may also be spotted here. Someone is usually always busy in two or three workshops. Car park and the cashier are located west of the street. *Tue–Sat 10am–6pm | at the southern end of town | admission 5 euros, children 2.50 euros*

Animal residents at the outdoor museum La Alcogida

CAMEL RIDES (127 E2) (*M H2*)

The *camel safaris* take place at the Corralejo dunes. The trip starts at the beach near the Hotel *Ríu Oliva Beach.* A roundtrip on these "ships of the desert" takes about 20 minutes. *Daily 11am–5pm | adults 7 euros, children 6 euros*

THE CENTRE

GO-CART TRACK OCIOS DEL SUR
(134 B4) (*M C10*)

There are three loop tracks (125 m/ 410 ft, 500 m/1,540 ft and 1,500 m/ 4,920 ft long) as well as a cafeteria for refreshments. *Daily 10am–7pm, during summer 11am–8pm | 10 min 18 euros, youths 12 euros, children 9 euros | approach from the FV 618 from the south to Cardón (turn left at the go-cart sign)*

OASIS PARK ★ (134 B5) (*M C12*)

Chimpanzees, otters, kangaroos, hippos, ostriches, marabou storks, flamingos, giraffes and other animals are all part of the attraction of this amazing park. Do not miss out on the entertaining animal shows with reptiles, parrots, sea lions and birds of prey. Children can get even closer to the animals on the kids' farm. A INSIDER TIP swaying ride on a camel is a lot of fun. Head off from zone 1 to a ☆ viewpoint on a hill above the sea (from zone 2: safari within the zoo). *Daily 9am–6pm | admission 33 euros, children 19.50 euros, camel ride 12, children 8 euros | on the FV 2 at La Lajita; there are also free buses from Morro Jable, Esquinzo, Costa Calma, Caleta de Fustes and Corralejo | information tel. 9 28 16 11 02 | www. fuerteventuraoasispark.com*

HIKING FROM AJUY TO CALETA NEGRA
(128 B3) (*M C8*)

The short hike to the mysterious "pirate caves" is an ideal outing for older children

A child all dressed up for some carnival fun

(from 8 years). The route is described in the "The Centre" chapter under Pájara/ Ajuy (see p. 67).

THE SOUTH

WALKS ON THE BEACH
(133 D6, E5) (*M A13–14*)

For older children, the beach hikes on the coast between Jandía Playa and the start of the lagoon are a lot of fun. The best time is during low tide early in the morning or in the early evening, when you can also do some bird watching.

FESTIVALS & EVENTS

Every town celebrates its patron saint day with processions, music and dancing. The highlights are the balls *(verbenas)* on the weekend before or after the main date.

JANUARY/FEBRUARY
Valle de Santa Inés (21 Jan); *Gran Tarajal* (2 Feb)

FEBRUARY/MARCH
★ ● *Carnival:* The majority of events take place in *Puerto del Rosario* and the prelude is a masked ball. Further balls follow, amongst them the *Verbena de la Sabana*, where the men wear wigs and dress in drag. High point: the procession in the evening (Sat/Sun)

MARCH/APRIL
Semana Santa/Easter: Processions with images of Mary and Christ

MAY
Tefía (4th); *Tarajalejo* (8th); *La Lajita* (13th)

MAY/JUNE
Corpus Christi: In *Puerto del Rosario* procession over "flower" carpets made from coloured stones

JUNE
Lajares (13th); *Ajuy* (24th); *Vallebrón* (24th); *Las Playitas* (29th)

JULY
Pájara (2nd)
During the *Día de San Buenaventura* (14th) in *Betancuria,* drummers and pipers celebrate the Castilian conquest of the island.
Fiesta Nuestra Señora del Carmen (16th) is celebrated in *Corralejo* with a parade and ★ *boat procession,* similarly in Morro Jable. Carmen is the patron saint of fishermen and sailors.
Casillas del Angel (26th)

AUGUST
Tetir (4th); *Tiscamanita* (3rd Sun); *Tindaya* (15th); *El Cotillo* (approx. 22nd); *Tefía* (28th)

SEPTEMBER
Antigua (8th); *Vega de Río de las Palmas* (3rd Sat): On Friday night pilgrims cross the mountain to Vega Río Palma, where a shrine houses the statue of the Virgen de la Peña, the island's patron saint. The following *Fiesta de la Peña fiesta* then goes on for over 40 hours.

The fun only really begins at midnight when the numerous fiestas start the festivities in honour of the local patron saints

OCTOBER

La Oliva (7th); The ★ *Fiesta Nuestra Señora del Rosario* in Puerto del Rosario is the largest fiesta on the island; procession with elaborate costumes and music. *Festival of St Michael* in Tuineje (13th): INSIDER TIP historical spectacle about the battle of Tamacite and the victory over English pirates.
La Ampuyenta (19th)

NOVEMBER/DECEMBER

Tetir (30 Nov); *Betancuria* (8 Dec)

EVENTS

The *Canary Islands Music Festival* (Jan–early Feb) also stops on Fuerteventura with many concerts. At the *Fuerteventura en Música* (end of June/beginning of July), bands play at the lagoons north of Cotillo – great atmosphere. In May at the wrestling arena in La Antigua artisans present their crafts at *Feria Insular de Artesanía* for a week. The highlight of the year is the ● ★ *Windsurfing World Cup* in front of the lagoon of Playa Barca mid/end of July – a two-week beach party! During November people meet in Corralejo for the *International Kite Festival.*

NATIONAL HOLIDAYS

1 Jan	New Year's Day
6 Jan	Epiphany
March/April	Holy Thursday, Good Friday
1 May	Labour Day
30 May	Canaries Day; Corpus Christi
25 July	St John's Day
15 Aug	Assumption
12 Oct	National Day
1 Nov	All Saints' Day
6 Dec	Constitution Day
8 Dec	Immaculate Conception
25 Dec	Christmas Day

LINKS, BLOGS, APPS & MORE

LINKS & BLOGS

www.spiritoffuerteventura.com This is a local English online magazine that not only has up-to-date island news but also offers all sorts of information about the best places to visit, excursions, cocktail bars, weather, videos and much more

www.fuerteventuraclick.com Platform-independent, smartphone-optimized site designed by the tourist board in several languages

www.fuertenews.com Another English language online weekly magazine with news, classifieds and useful sections like "Fun Stuff" and "Island Information"

visitfuerteventura.es/en Official site with information on anything, ranging from nature parks, gay friendly places and the best spas to practical travel information

www.hellocanaryislands.com/fuerteventura Website for all Canary Islands with little information, but large and fascinating photographs -- to get you into the mood quickly

www.facebook.com/ifuerteventura The island's facebook page has all the latest tips on events, nightlife, sports and more

www.alohasurfacademy.com Blog by the owners of a surf school in Corralejo with entries about yoga retreats, surf classes, volcano hikes and island tours

www.canarynightlife.net/forum An online open forum that discusses anything and everything about the bars, restaurants and nightlife on the island

www.fuerteventura-forum.com Discussion groups with various categories and topics

casadelaburra.wordpress.com A Spanish blog by the owner of a holiday home that details important cultural and tourist events on the island

Regardless of whether you are still researching your trip or already on Fuerteventura: these addresses will provide you with more information, videos and networks to make your holiday even more enjoyable

www.fuerteventurarelocation.co.uk This blog is geared to expats who want to make the move to Fuerteventura but it is also full of useful tourist tips and information like where to find the best tapas, the late night chemist and the best accommodation

vimeo.com/channels/Fuerteventura A video site with about 27 posts of good quality videos

VIDEOS

www.rene-egli.com The island's top windsurfing centre has a video that gives you an excellent idea of what to expect on Fuerteventura

www.youtube.com/watch?v=6bzsmGy3VwI Here you can get a first glimpse of three of the best hiking routes on Fuerteventura

www.responsibletravel.com/Fuerteventura-Travel-Guide/Fuerteventura-Podcasts.htm A very interesting series of podcasts from island locals (in English) that are grouped into categories like "Nature & Wildlife", "Culture & History" and "Food"

Fuerte Amador Travel guide and offline map. An advantage: detailed vector maps that are updated based on OpenStreetMap

APPS

Islas Canarias Water Sports Experience Infos on windsurfing, sailing and other water sports (iPad)

Top 10 Fuerteventura Varied information on everything important – from car rentals to events (Androis and iPhone)

iTranslate A free translation tool – type in a phrase and hear it translated back to you in Spanish – very handy when you need to order food or ask for directions

TRAVEL TIPS

ARRIVAL

There are a large number of budget and charter companies that offer direct flights from the UK to Fuerteventura. With such a selection it is simply a matter of comparing prices and hunting for the best deal. In the UK, British Airways, Easyjet, Thomas Cook, Norwegian, Ryanair and TUI fly from London; there are also flights from many more places such as Manchester, Liverpool, Newcastle or Edinburgh. Most travel agents have very reasonable flat-rate package deals that include flight and accommodation. For those travelling from outside of the UK the best option would be to transfer at one of the major European airports like London or Madrid. Spain, France and the Netherlands also have direct flights on their national carriers. On arrival on Fuerteventura, the transport from the airport to the holiday destinations is usually included in the package. There are many car rental companies with counters at the airport. Their cars can then be found at the numbered parking spots on the right (northern) end of the airport parking lot.

Fuerteventura has no direct ferry connections. Coming from Cadíz, you have to change over on one of the other Canary Islands. There is only a connection once or twice a week. For two people with a passenger car you can expect to pay at least 1,500 euros. Information and reservations for ferry passage at travel agents or directly at *www.trasmediterranea.es* or *www.navieraarmas.com*.

BANKS & CREDIT CARDS

During the week, banks are mostly open from 8:30am–2pm, Saturdays until 12:30 or 1pm. You can draw money from ATMs using a Visa card, MasterCard, EC and debit card.

Major credit cards are accepted by many banks, hotels, car rental companies as well as in shops and restaurants.

BUSES

There are 17 bus lines that connect all the large towns. The lines most relevant to tourists are lines 1 and 10 (Morro Jable/Costa Calma–capital, mostly hourly), line 3 (Caleta de Fustes–capital, mostly half-hourly), line 5 (Morro Jable–Costa Calma, mostly hourly), line 6 (Corralejo–capital, mostly half-hourly), line 7 (Cotillo–capital, three times daily), line 8 (Corralejo–

RESPONSIBLE TRAVEL

It doesn't take a lot to be environmentally friendly whilst travelling. Don't just think about your carbon footprint whilst flying to and from your holiday destination but also about how you can protect nature and culture abroad. As a tourist it is especially important to respect nature, look out for local products, cycle instead of driving, save water and much more. If you would like to find out more about eco-tourism please visit: *www.ecotourism.org*

Cotillo, mostly hourly) and line 25 (Morro Jable/Costa Calma—Oasis Park, mostly hourly). Lines 3 and 10 stop at the airport.

CAMPING

The official campsites have no amenities (toilets, showers, water, etc.) and to use them you are required to register in the town hall of the relevant community where you also need to pay a deposit. Maximum duration of stay in nature reserves is seven days, outside of campsites 24 hours (with a permit as well).

CAR & CAR HIRE

An international license is not essential as national licenses are accepted. For more information about the traffic regulations see *www.canaryuk.com/driving. html*. Buckling up is required by law and the speed limit for passenger cars in the towns is 50 km/h and 90 km/h on the country roads. The blood-alcohol limit is 0.25 and the Spanish police have zero tolerance. On Fuerteventura there are often roadblocks, especially at night and during weekends.

There is a wide choice of rental cars available in the holiday resorts and at the airport. Three day and weekly rates are the best. A small rental car starts at 130 euros per week, an off-road vehicle at about 70 euros per day. Ensure that unlimited mileage, collision damage waiver and full personal accident insurance are included in the price. To hire a car the minimum age is 21 (at some companies it is even 23). During the high season you will need to book in advance. You do not need an off-road vehicle for normal travel around the island, but if you want to drive on the byways and gravel roads an off-road vehicle is recommended. Remember that most of the time this is excluded from the accident insurance of normal rental cars. Irrespective of the matter of insurance, off-road jeeps are always recommended if you're planning tours to the westerly point and Cofete.

CONSULATES & EMBASSIES

BRITISH CONSULATE ON FUERTEVENTURA

A British consular officer makes routine visits to Fuerteventura and is available for assistance and advice at: *Hotel Barcelo Corralejo Bay | Av. Grandes Playas 12 | Corralejo | La Oliva | 35660 Fuerteventura | tel. +349 02 10 93 56 | ukinspain.fco.gov. uk/en*

AMERICAN CONSULAR AGENCY IN LAS PALMAS

Edificio ARCA | C/ Los Martinez de Escobar 3 | 35007 Las Palmas | tel. +349 28 27 12 59 | madrid.usembassy.gov/citizen-servi ces/offices/las-palmas.html

CUSTOMS

The Canaries is a free trade zone without customs control. UK citizens do not have to pay any duty on goods brought from another EU country as long as tax was included in the price and they are for private consumption. The limits are: 800 cigarettes, 400 cigarillo, 200 cigars, 1kg smoking tobacco, 10L spirits, 20L liqueurs, 90L wine, 110L beer.

Travellers from the USA, Canada, Australia or other non-EU countries are allowed to enter with the following tax-free amounts: 200 cigarettes or 100 cigarillos or 50 cigars or 250g smoking tobacco. 2L wine and spirits with less 22 vol % alcohol, 1L spirits with more than 22vol % alcohol content.

Travellers to the United States who are returning residents of the country do not have to pay duty on articles purchased overseas up to the value of $800, but there are limits on the amount of alcoholic beverages and tobacco products. For the regulations for international travel for US residents please see *www.cbp.gov*

CYCLING PATHS

There are only 47 km/29 miles of paved bicycle paths on the entire island, the "rest" of the signposted paths are off-road trails *(visitfuerteventura.es/rutas-ciclistas)*. Racing cyclists have to share most roads with cars. The older island roads are narrow and local drivers have little regard for cyclists.

ELECTRICITY

200 Volts. Adapters are needed for UK appliances.

EMERGENCY SERVICES

Dial *112* for the police, ambulance and fire brigade. Or contact your hotel for help.

FERRIES

Two ferry lines offer trips from Corralejo to Lanzarote/Playa Blanca daily, up to 14 trips (travelling time 25 minutes, price per trip from 14 euros, car transport from 36 euros). *Líneas Fred Olsen*

(tel. 9 02 10 01 07 | www.fredolsen.es) and *Naviera Armas (tel. 9 02 45 65 00 | www.navieraarmas.com)*.

Both companies offer car ferries from Morro Jable to Las Palmas de Gran Canaria (3 times daily, travel time from 2 hours) with connection to Tenerife.

FLIGHT CONNECTIONS

There are a dozen daily flight connections to Las Palmas on Gran Canaria and up to four to Tenerife/Los Rodeos, several times a week to Madrid. No connections to other Canary Islands. Bookings and information: *Binter (tel. 9 02 39 13 92 | www.binternet.com)*. More flight information *tel. airport 9 02 40 47 04*.

HEALTH

Holidaymakers with a European Health Insurance Card (EHIC) issued by your social-security office will be treated free of charge in casualty wards and hospitals associated with the Spanish *Seguridad Social*. In other cases, you should make sure that you receive a detailed receipt for any treatment received to be able to claim a refund when you return home.

DOCTORS

For a list of English speaking doctors see: *http://ukinspain.fco.gov.uk/en/about-us/other-locations/las-palmas-consulate/local-contacts* and download "Doctors on Fuerteventura" pdf.

CHEMISTS

Farmacías can be found in all the large holiday resorts and in Esquinzo, Puerto del Rosario and Gran Tarajal.
Medication is often cheaper than at home.

IMMIGRATION

Citizens of the UK and Ireland, USA, Canada, Australia and New Zealand need only a valid passport to enter all EU countries. Children under the age of 12 need a children's passport.

INFORMATION IN ADVANCE

For online information and to order brochures see: *www.spain.info/en_GB/*

SPANISH TOURIST BOARD OFFICES
6th floor | 64 North Row | London | W1K 7DE | tel. 020 73 17 20 11 | www.spain.info/en_GB/
60 East 42nd Street | suite 53000 53rd floor | New York | tel. +1 212 265 88 22 | www.spain.info/en_US/

INFORMATION ON FUERTEVENTURA

PATRONATO DE TURISMO
C/ Almirante Lallermand 1 | Puerto del Rosario | opposite the pier | tel. 9 28 53 08 44 | visitfuerteventura.es/en |

INTERNET

Classic Internet cafes have virtually died out now what with the spread of smartphones and many bars in all tourist towns offering free WiFi (just ask for the password). By now, most hotels have also begun to offer free WiFi to their guests, but especially in the larger resorts, connections are often reeeaally slow.

NUDISM

Bathing naked is a no-no on city beaches and in the vicinity of buildings; on many other beaches it is common and will be tolerated.

OPENING HOURS

Shops are usually open during the week between 9am and 1pm and 5pm–8pm, in the holiday resorts they often also stay open on weekends. Restaurants often observe a siesta from 3 to 6pm.

PHONE & MOBILE PHONE

Since the end of roaming charges within Europe in mid-2017, telephoning in Spain has become cheaper. It costs a maximum of 3.2 cents per minute to call and there is a cap of 7.70 euros per GB for data. Generally it's no longer worth buying a

CURRENCY CONVERTER

£	€	€	£
1	1.14	1	0.88
3	3.43	3	2.63
5	5.70	5	4.38
13	14.85	13	11.38
40	46	40	35
75	86	75	66
120	137	120	105
250	286	250	219
500	571	500	438

$	€	€	$
1	0.81	1	1.23
3	2.43	3	3.70
5	4.05	5	6.17
13	10.54	13	16.04
40	32.42	40	49.35
75	61	75	92.52
120	97	120	148
250	203	250	308
500	405	500	617

For current exchange rates see www.xe.com

Spanish SIM card or using Spanish phone cards called *teletarjetas*. International call shops, known in Spain as *locutorios*, are only an option if you're calling outside Europe and WiFi and Skype are not an option. However there are special roaming regulations which apply to Spain but which cannot be described here in detail. *Dialling code to the UK: 0044, to the US: 001; to Spain: 0034.* Your mobile phone will automatically choose a Spanish network.

POST

There are post offices in Corralejo, Costa Calma, Gran Tarajal and Morro Jable *(Mon–Sat until noon)* as well as in Puerto del Rosario *(Mon–Fri 8:30am–8:30pm, Sat 9:30am–1pm)*. Stamps are usually also available at hotel receptions, these stamps are from private postal companies so do not post your mail in the usual public letterboxes but hand them in at the same place where you purchased the stamps. Postcards and standard letters to the EU cost 1.25 euros.

BUDGETING

Camel rides	£ 10.50/$ 15 *children £ 7/$ 10*
Beach lounger	£ 10.50/$ 15 *for two loungers with parasols per day*
Car hire	from £ 53/$ 75 *for three days*
Windsurfing	£140/$ 200 *for a six-hour-beginner's course*
Petrol	£ 0.97/$ 1.34 *per litre regular*
Island tour	£ 44/$ 62 *with bus and guide*

PRICES

Prices on Fuerteventura are generally on par with those in the rest of Europe. A simple lunch in the most affordable restaurant is about 9 euros while a restaurant dinner will set you back 15 to 25 euros per person. There are no fees to access any of the beaches but you will need to pay if you want the use of deckchairs and umbrellas. Alcohol, tobacco and petrol are cheaper than at home.

SMOKING

Spanish legislature has banned smoking in restaurants unless they have a separate smoking room. The problem is a theoretical one since most guests sit outside anyway.

TAXI

The basic rate on weekdays 6am–10pm is 3.05 euros and 0.53 euros is added per kilometre; evenings and holidays 3.35 euro plus 0.60 euro per kilometre.

TIME

Fuerteventura has GMT all year round (simultaneous switching to winter or summer time). The North American east coast is 5 hours behind, the west coast 8 hours.

TIPPING

To tip waiters and taxi drivers, you can round up the bill by 5 per cent. For chambermaids 3 euros is recommended at the beginning and thereafter every four to five days depending on how happy you are with the service. For other services, small tips are also customary.

WATER

Drinking water is sold everywhere in plastic bottles or canisters. Although the tap water is safe, it comes mainly from desalination plants and is suitable for drinking and cooking only to a limited extent.

WHEN TO GO & WHAT TO WEAR

Fuerteventura's season is year-round. However, the air and water temperatures are most pleasant in autumn. During mid-summer, the sun and constant strong winds can be unpleasant for those with a sensitive nature and small children (swirling sand on the beach!). From January to April it can be cool and the water temperatures are too cold to swim. Always take along long trousers, a jacket as well as a jersey during the winter and spring as the evenings can be chilly. The main season prices usually apply to July/August and Christmas. During August, many restaurants close for the summer holidays.

WEATHER ON FUERTEVENTURA

	Jan	Feb	March	April	May	June	July	Aug	Sept	Oct	Nov.	Dec
Daytime temperatures in °C/°F	19/66	19/66	20/68	21/70	23/73	24/75	27/81	27/81	26/79	24/75	21/70	19/66
Nighttime temperatures in °C/°F	12/54	12/54	13/55	13/55	15/59	16/61	18/64	19/66	18/64	17/63	15/59	13/55
Sunshine hours/day	6	7	8	8	9	9	10	10	8	7	6	6
Precipitation days/month	3	2	1	1	1	0	0	0	0	1	3	3
Water temperature in °C/°F	18/64	18/64	17/63	17/63	18/64	20/68	20/68	21/70	22/72	22/72	20/68	19/66

USEFUL PHRASES SPANISH

PRONUNCIATION

c	before "e" and "i" like "th" in "thin"
ch	as in English
g	before "e" and "i" like the "ch" in Scottish "loch"
gue, gui	like "get", "give"
que, qui	the "u" is not spoken, i.e. "ke", "ki"
j	always like the "ch" in Scottish "loch"
ll	like "lli" in "million"; some speak it like "y" in "yet"
ñ	"nj"
z	like "th" in "thin"

IN BRIEF

Yes/No/Maybe	sí/no/quizás
Please/Thank you	por favor/gracias
Hello!/Goodbye!/See you	¡Hola!/¡Adiós!/¡Hasta luego!
Good morning!/afternoon!/evening!/night!	¡Buenos días!/¡Buenos días!/¡Buenas tardes!/¡Buenas noches!
Excuse me, please!	¡Perdona!/¡Perdone!
May I...?/Pardon?	¿Puedo...?/¿Cómo dice?
My name is...	Me llamo...
What's your name?	¿Cómo se llama usted?/¿Cómo te llamas?
I'm from...	Soy de...
I would like to.../Have you got...?	Querría.../¿Tiene usted...?
How much is...?	¿Cuánto cuesta...?
I (don't) like that	Esto (no) me gusta.
good/bad/broken/doesn't work	bien/mal/roto/no funciona
too much/much/little/all/nothing	demasiado/mucho/poco/todo/nada
Help!/Attention!/Caution!	¡Socorro!/¡Atención!/¡Cuidado!
ambulance/police/fire brigade	ambulancia/policía/bomberos
May I take a photo here	¿Podría fotografiar aquí?

DATE & TIME

Monday/Tuesday/Wednesday	lunes/martes/miércoles
Thursday/Friday/Saturday	jueves/viernes/sábado
Sunday/working day/holiday	domingo/laborable/festivo
today/tomorrow/yesterday	hoy/mañana/ayer

¿Hablas español?

"Do you speak Spanish?" This guide will help you to say the basic words and phrases in Spanish

hour/minute/second/moment	hora/minuto/segundo/momento
day/night/week/month/year	día/noche/semana/mes/año
now/immediately/before/after	ahora/enseguida/antes/después
What time is it?	¿Qué hora es?
It's three o'clock/It's half past three	Son las tres/Son las tres y media
a quarter to four/a quarter past four	cuatro menos cuarto/ cuatro y cuarto

TRAVEL

open/closed/opening times	abierto/cerrado/horario
entrance/exit	entrada/acceso salida
departure/arrival	salida/llegada
toilets/ladies/gentlemen	aseos/señoras/caballeros
free/occupied	libre/ocupado
(not) drinking water	agua (no) potable
Where is...?/Where are...?	¿Dónde está...? /¿Dónde están...?
left/right	izquierda/derecha
straight ahead/back	recto/atrás
close/far	cerca/lejos
traffic lights/corner/crossing	semáforo/esquina/cruce
bus/tram/U underground/ taxi/cab	autobús/tranvía/metro/ taxi
bus stop/cab stand	parada/parada de taxis
parking lot/parking garage	parking/garaje
street map/map	plano de la ciudad/mapa
train station/harbour/airport	estación/puerto/aeropuerto
ferry/quay	transbordador/muelle
schedule/ticket/supplement	horario/billete/suplemento
single/return	sencillo/ida y vuelta
train/track/platform	tren/vía/andén
delay/strike	retraso/huelga
I would like to rent...	Querría... alquilar
a car/a bicycle/a boat	un coche/una bicicleta/un barco
petrol/gas station	gasolinera
petrol/gas / diesel	gasolina/diesel
breakdown/repair shop	avería/taller

FOOD & DRINK

Could you please book a table for tonight for four?	Resérvenos, por favor, una mesa para cuatro personas para hoy por la noche.
on the terrace/by the window	en la terraza/junto a la ventana

The menu, please/	¡El menú, por favor!
Could I please have...?	¿Podría traerme... por favor?
bottle/carafe/glass	botella/jarra/vaso
knife/fork/spoon	cuchillo/tenedor/cuchara
salt/pepper/sugar	sal/pimienta/azúcar
vinegar/oil/milk/cream/lemon	vinagre/aceite/leche/limón
cold/too salty/not cooked	frío/demasiado salado/sin hacer
with/without ice/sparkling	con/sin hielo/gas
vegetarian/allergy	vegetariano/vegetariana/alergía
May I have the bill, please?	Querría pagar, por favor
bill/receipt/tip	cuenta/recibo/propina

SHOPPING

pharmacy/chemist	farmacia/droguería
baker/market	panadería/mercado
butcher/fishmonger	carnicería/pescadería
shopping centre/department store	centro comercial/grandes almacenes
shop/supermarket/kiosk	tienda/supermercado/quiosco
100 grammes/1 kilo	cien gramos/un kilo
expensive/cheap/price/more/less	caro/barato/precio/más/menos
organically grown	de cultivo ecológico

ACCOMMODATION

I have booked a room	He reservado una habitación.
Do you have any... left?	¿Tiene todavía...?
single room/double room	habitación individual/habitación doble
breakfast/half board/	desayuno/media pensión/
full board (American plan)	pensión completa
at the front/seafront/garden view	hacia delante/hacia el mar/hacia el jardín
shower/sit-down bath	ducha/baño
balcony/terrace	balcón/terraza
key/room card	llave/tarjeta
luggage/suitcase/bag	equipaje/maleta/bolso
swimming pool/spa/sauna	piscina/spa/sauna
soap/toilet paper/nappy (diaper)	jabón/papel higiénico/pañal
cot/high chair/nappy changing	cuna/trona/cambiar los pañales
deposit	anticipo/caución

BANKS, MONEY & CREDIT CARDS

bank/ATM/	banco/cajero automático/
pin code	número secreto
cash/credit card	en efectivo/tarjeta de crédito
bill/coin/change	billete/moneda/cambio

HEALTH

doctor/dentist/paediatrician	médico/dentista/pediatra
hospital/emergency clinic	hospital/urgencias
fever/pain/inflamed/injured	fiebre/dolor/inflamado/herido
diarrhoea/nausea/sunburn	diarrea/náusea/quemadura de sol
plaster/bandage/ointment/cream	tirita/vendaje/pomada/crema
pain reliever/tablet/suppository	calmante/comprimido/supositorio

POST, TELECOMMUNICATIONS & MEDIA

stamp/letter/postcard	sello/carta/postal
I need a landline phone card/	Necesito una tarjeta telefónica/
I'm looking for a prepaid card for my mobile	Busco una tarjeta prepago para mi móvil
Where can I find internet access?	¿Dónde encuentro un acceso a internet?
dial/connection/engaged	marcar/conexión/ocupado
socket/adapter/charger	enchufe/adaptador/cargador
computer/battery/	ordenador/batería/
rechargeable battery	batería recargable
e-mail address/at sign (@)	(dirección de) correo electrónico/arroba
internet address (URL)	dirección de internet
internet connection/wifi	conexión a internet/wifi
e-mail/file/print	archivo/imprimir

LEISURE, SPORTS & BEACH

beach/sunshade/lounger	playa/sombrilla/tumbona
low tide/high tide/current	marea baja/marea alta/corriente

NUMBERS

0	cero	14	catorce
1	un, uno, una	15	quince
2	dos	16	dieciséis
3	tres	17	diecisiete
4	cuatro	18	dieciocho
5	cinco	19	diecinueve
6	seis	20	veinte
7	siete	100	cien, ciento
8	ocho	200	doscientos, doscientas
9	nueve	1000	mil
10	diez	2000	dos mil
11	once	10000	diez mil
12	doce	1/2	medio
13	trece	1/4	un cuarto

ROAD ATLAS

The green line indicates the Discovery Tour "Fuerteventura at a glance"
The blue line indicates the other Discovery Tours

All tours are also marked on the pull-out map

Exploring Fuerteventura

The map on the back cover shows how the area has been sub-divided

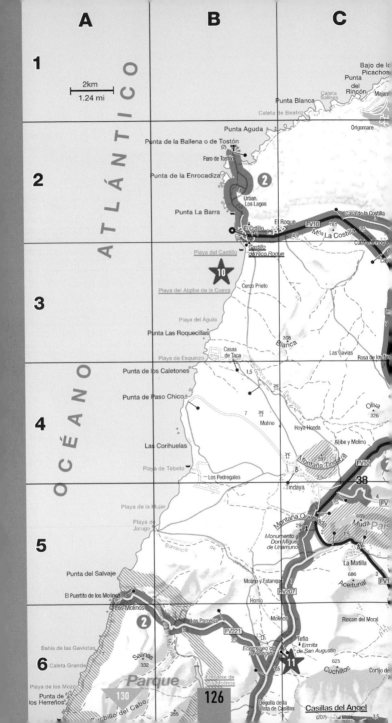

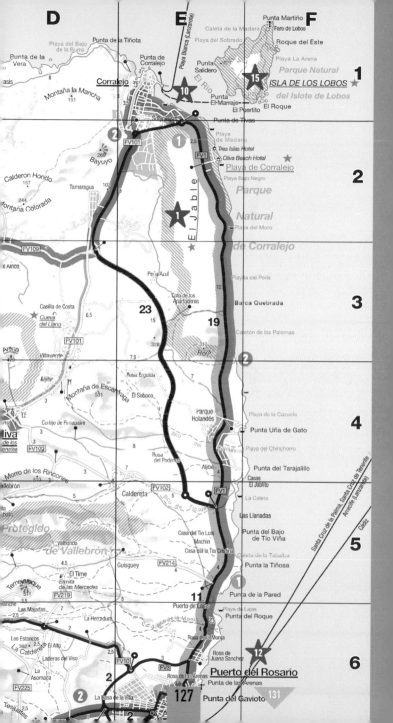

D

Playa del Bajo
de la Burra
Punta de la Tiñota
Punta de la Vera
asis
8
Montaña la Mancha
151
Corralejo
3,5
269
FV101
Bayuyo
Calderon Hondo
157
Tamaragua
103
244
Montaña Colorada

E

Punta de Corralejo
Punta Salidero
Punta El-Marrajo
127
El Puertito
El Roque
Punta de Tivas
Playa de Medano
Tres Islas Hotel
Oliva Beach Hotel
Playa de Corralejo
Playa Bajo Negro

Playa Blanca (Lanzarote)
Playa del Sobrado

F

Punta Martiño
Faro de Lobos
Caleta de la Madera
Roque del Este
Playa La Arena
Parque Natural
ISLA DE LOS LOBOS
del Islote de Lobos

10
15

1

2

Parque

Natural

de Corralejo

El Jable

1

Playa del Moro

FV1

FV109
5
e Arriba

Casilla de Costa
Cueva del Llano
6,5
FV101
Villaverde
Arena
450
7,5

23
15
328

Peña Azul
Coto de los Apartadrron
312
Roja

Playa del Poris
Barca Quebrada
Caletón de las Palomas

12

19

2

3

Aljibe
3
Montaña de Escanfraga
531
El Sobaco
Rosa Ergulula

Corrillo de Fimapaire
FV102
3
Morro de los Rincones
allebrón
5

8

iva
de los
enales

Rosa del Poderica
7

Parque Holandés

7

Aljibe

Playa de la Cazuola
Punta Uña de Gato
Playa del Chinchorro

Punta del Tarajalillo
Casas
El Jablito
La Caleta

FV102
Caldereta
FV1
bco. de Tisoh

4

Protegido
de Vallebrón
la bello
Valhondo
4,5
El Time
Ermita de las Mercedes
FV219
Temejereque
5,1
Guisguey
FV214

Casa del Tío Luis
Machín
Casa de la Tía Cristina

Las Llanadas
Punta del Bajo de Tío Viña
Caleta de la Tabalta
Punta la Tiñosa

Santa Cruz de la Palma Santa Cruz de Tenerife
Arrecife (Lanzarote)

5

Cadiz

3,5
mariche
Las Majadas
2,5
La Herradura

Los Estancos
392
El Alto
La Caldereta
Laderas del Viso
La Asomada
FV225
Tesfuiaes
2,5

8

11

Puerto de Lajas
Rosa de la Monja

4

4

Punta de la Pared
Playa de Lajas
Punta del Roque

1

FV10
2
2
La Rosa de la Villa

FV3
Rosa de las Arenas
3,5
127
131

Rosa de Juana Sanchez

12

Puerto del Rosario
Punta de las Arenas
Punta del Gavioto

6

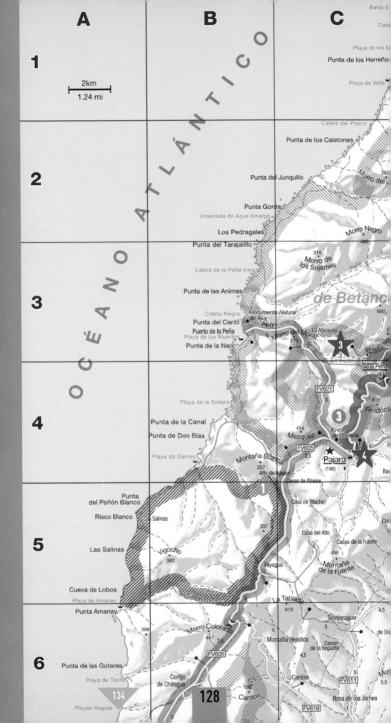

	A	B	C

1

Bahía d

Cale

Playa de los M

Punta de los Herreño

Playa de Valle

2km
1.24 mi

2

Caleta del Pasco

Punta de los Caletones

Punta del Junquillo

282

Morro del

Punta Gorda

Ensenada de Agua Amarga

Morro Negro

Los Pedragales

480

Punta del Tarajalillo

3

316

Morro de
los Sojames

Caleta de la Peña Vieja

Barranco

de Betanc

Punta de las Ánimas

660

Caleta Negra

Monumento Natural
de Ajuy

Punta del Cantil

Ajuy

La Atalayeja

Puerto de la Peña

Morro del Moral

Playa de los Muertos

213

Embalse

Punta de la Nao

Emba
de la Peña

4

FV621

Playa de la Solapa

5

619

Féndúc

Punta de la Canal

414

Finca
de la Navia

Punta de Don Blas

Mezquez

FV605

Playa de Garcey

Montaña Blanca

2.5

Pajara

(196)

257

Alto de Aguaje

Ba

Casas de Abaise

5

Punta
del Peñón Blanco

Casa de Machin

Risco Blanco

La Salinas

337

Casa del Alto

Cor

Las Salinas

Vigocho

Casas de la Fuente

382

496

Fayagua

Montaña
de la Fuente

Cueva de Lobos

Playa de Amanay

La Tablada

Punta Amanay

619

Tesejerague

de Di

306

Morro Colorado

5

447

2.5

Montaña Hendida

Casas
de la Vegueta

4.5

6

Punta de las Goteras

FV605

Cardón

5

Playa de Terife

51

FV611

5.5

Mo

134

Cortijo
de Chilegua

128

Rosa de los Jarnes

Playas Negras

Cardón

FV618

5

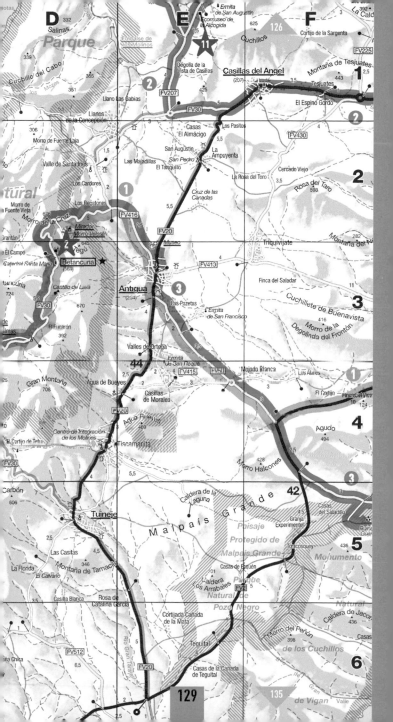

D

Salinas
332
Parque
339
Embalse de los Molinos
Cuchillo del Cabo
355
351
5,5
Llanos
de la Concepción
306
Morro de Fuente Laja
1,5
Valle de Santa Inés
tural
Los Cardones 2
Morro de
la Fuente Vieja
Los Regaderos
Morro de la Cruz
FV416
Mirador
Morro Velosa
Grantán
El Campo
Catedral Santa María
645
Betancuria ★
Betancuria
724
Castillo de Lara
tancuria
FV30
670
de
El Bucarón
limas
392

E

Ermita
de San Augustín
Corruseo de
la Alcogida
1,5
11
Llano las Gabias
FV207
Casas
El Almácigo
San Augustín
Las Majadillas
San Pedro
El Tanquillo
Cruz de las
Cañadas
5,5
Museo
5
3
Antigua
(264)
Las Pozetas
4
2
Valles de Ortega
Ermita
de San Roque
44
2,5
FV415
FV50

F

La Cald
392
Cortijo de la Sargenta
126
FV225
Montaña de Tesjuates
443
Tesjuates 1 2,5
Casillas del Angel
(207)
3,5
El Espino Gordo
2
FV430
La Ampuyenta
La Rosa del Toro
Cercado Viejo
3,5
Rosa del Taro
593
2
282
Montaña del N
Triquivijate
FV413
4
Finca del Saladar
11
Cuchillete de Buenavista
416
Morro de la
Degollada del Frontón
3
Ermita
de San Francisco

Majada Blanca
Los Alares
1
3
El Cortijo
Finca del Vica
10 124
Agudo
494
4
3
Morro Halcones
428
3
Gran Montaña
708
Agua de Bueyes
25
Casillas
de Morales
FV20
Agua Burgos
369
Centro de Integración
de los Molinos
El Cortijo de Tetir
Tiscamanita
FV30
5,5

Carbón
606
7
Tuineje
2,5
Las Casitas 4,5
La Florida
346
Montaña de Tamacite
El Cavario
Casilla Blanca
3,5
Rosa de
Catalina García

Caldera de la
Laguna
Malpaís Grande
Paisaje
Protegido de
Malpaís Grande
Casas de Esquén
Caldera
Los Arrabales
FV2
Parque
Natural de
Pozo Negro

42
Granja
Experimental
Casas
del Saladillo
Torcosquey
436
5
Ruine
Guan
Monumento

ña Chita
FV512
6,5

Cortijada Cañada
de la Mata
Teguital
Casas de la Cañada
de Teguital
FV20
2

Río Gran Taraja
5

Morro del Peñón
398
de los Cuchillos

Natural
Caldera de Jacor
436
Casas
6
Gran
de Vigan Valle

129

135

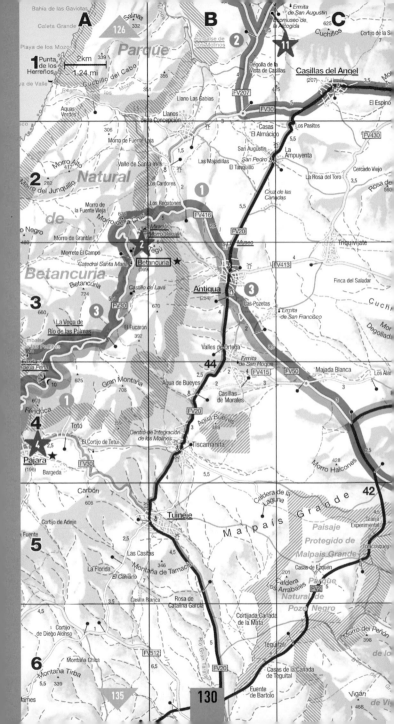

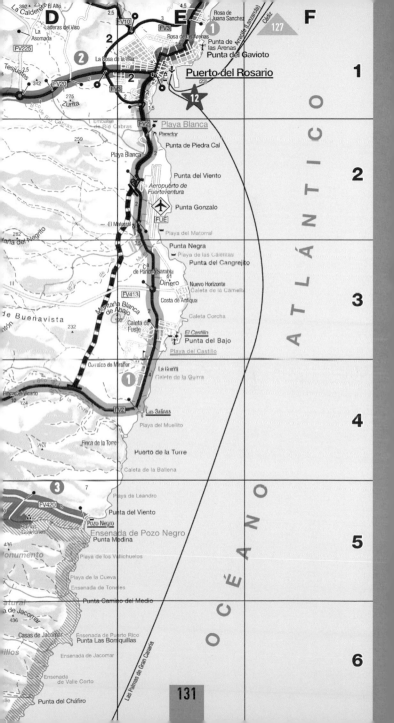

La Calderata El Alto
Laderas del Viso
La Asomada
FV225
Tejuates
342
FV20
275
Zurita

FV10
FV3
Rosa de
Juana Sanchez
Rosa de Las Arenas
La Rosa de la Villa
Punta de
las Arenas
Punta del Gavioto

2

FV3

127

F

E

Puerto del Rosario

1

12

Embalse
de Río Cabras
FV2
259
Playa Blanca
Playa Blanca
Playa Blanca
Parador
Punta de Piedra Cal

Punta del Viento

Aeropuerto de
Fuerteventura
Punta Gonzalo
FUE

2

282
fiaña del Negro
El Matorral
Playa del Matorral

Punta Negra
Playa de las Caletas
Punta del Cangrejito

Ca
de Pancho Sarabia
61
Dinero

Nuevo Horizonte
Caleta de la Camella

FV413
Montaña Blanca
de Abajo
232
Caleta de
Fuste

Costa de Antigua

Caleta Corcha

3

de Buenavista

El Castillo
Punta del Bajo
Playa del Castillo

Corrales de Miraflor

1

La Guirra
Caleta de la Guirra

Finca del Pinario
10   124

FV2

Las Salinas

Playa del Muellito

4

Finca de la Torre

Puerto de la Torre

Caleta de la Ballena

3

FV420

Playa de Leandro

Punta del Viento

aunas
Guanches

Pozo Negro

Ensenada de Pozo Negro
Punta Medina

436

5

onumento

Playa de los Vallichuelos

Playa de la Cueva
Ensenada de Toneles

atural
a Jacomar
436

Punta Camino del Medio

Casas de Jacomar

Ensenada de Puerto Rico
Punta Las Bombquillas

illos

Ensenada de Jacomar

Las Palmas de Gran Canaria

6

Ensenada
de Valle Corto

Punta del Cháfiro

A   T   L   Á   N   T   I   C   O

O   C   É   A   N   O

OCÉANO ATL

A   **B**   **C**

1

2km
1.24 mi

2

3

4

Playa
EL ISLOTE

5

Punta Pesebre

Caleta de la Madera

Punta de Mal Rayo Punta de Barlovento

Roque del Moro

★ Playa de Cofete

Punta Cotillo o de Cachorros

Las Talahijas

189

Cofete

Fraile

Pico de

14

7

485

Playa de Ojos

4

M

Las Pilas

Casa y Manantial del Mosquito

424

Cuchillo del Palo

683

Casas de Gran Valle

de Ja

Punta del Tigre

Cuevа de la Negra

La Rajita

a

c

441

Morro Mungia

390

Puerto de la Cruz

Punta Salinas

Playa de las Pilas

Playa de Juan Gómez

i

z

o

d

e

7

Casas de Jorós

4

Punta de Jandía

Punta del Viento

6

Las Palmas de Gran Canaria

Santa Cruz de Tenerife

Puerto de la Cebaba

Morro Ja

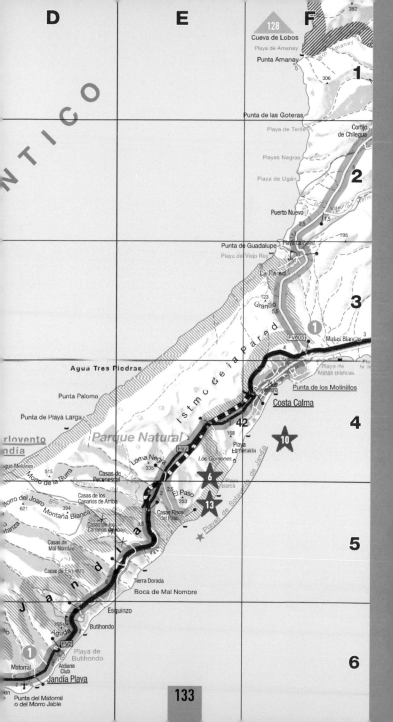

D E F

128
Cueva de Lobos
Playa de Amanay
Punta Amanay

382

1800 Amanay

306

1

Punta de las Goteras

Playa de Terife

Cortijo
de Chilegua

Playas Negras

Playa de Ugán

5

2

Puerto Nuevo

2,5   1,5

195

Punta de Guadalupe
Playa del Viejo Rey

Playa la Pared
↓

La Pared

123
Granillo
5,5

ATLÁNTICO

FV605   ①   Matas Blancas   3

3

Agua Tres Piedras

Playa de
Matas Blancas

Punta Paloma

Club
Salventura

Punta de los Molinillos

Costa Calma

Punta de Playa Larga

42

Parque Natural
Jandía

158

Playa
Esmeralda

★ 10

4

Agua Meliánes

Mono de la Burra

515

FV2

Los Gorriones

Loma Negra
335

Casas de
Pacenescal

★ 6

Barlovento
Jandía

Casas de los
Canarios de Arriba

2,5 El Paso
253

★ 13

Playa
Barca

Morro del Joaro

621

394

Montaña Blanca

Casas de los
Canarios de Abajo

3

Casas Risco
del Paso

★

Playas de Sotavento de Jandía

5

Matanza

Casas de
Mal Nombre

3,5

Casas de Esquinzo

Tierra Dorada

Boca de Mal Nombre

Esquinzo

Jandía

Butihondo
Águda

255,0

FV2

Playa de
Butihondo

① Matorral

Aldiana
Club

Jandía Playa

6

Punta del Matorral
o del Morro Jable

2

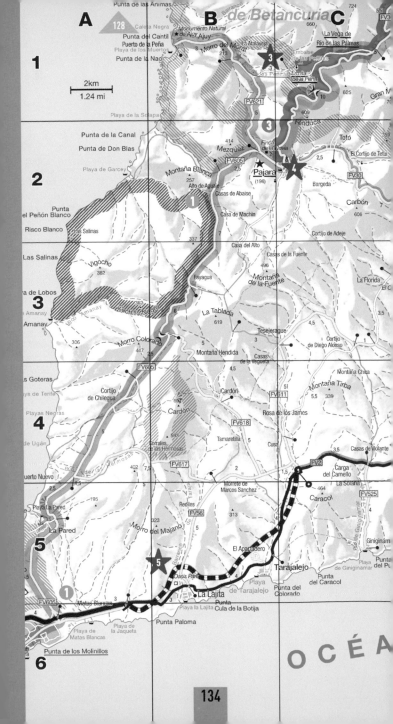

A
128

B de Betancuria **C**

Punta de las Ánimas

Caleta Negra

Monumento Natural
de Ajuy

Punta del Cantil
Puerto de a Peña
Playa de los Muertos
Punta de la Nao

1

2km
1.24 mi

La Atalayeja

Morro del Morán

213

Embalse
de las Peñitas

Ermita
de la Peña

La Vega de
Río de las Palmas

724

FV3

660

625

Gran M

70

Las Peñitas

Playa de la Solapa

Fenduca

609

Punta de la Canal

Punta de Don Blas

Mezquez

414

Finca
de la Vieja

Totó

El Cortijo de Tetu

Playa de Garcey

FV605

Montaña Blanca

257

Alto de Aguaje

Casas de Abaise

Casa de Machín

Pajara

(196)

2,5

Bargeda

FV30

Carbón

606

Punta
el Peñón Blanco

Risco Blanco

2

Las Salinas

Las Salinas

Vigocho

382

337

Casa del Alto

Casas de la Fuente

495

Fayagua

Montaña
de la-Fuente

La Florida

El C

a de Lobos

Amanay

Amanay

306

Cuchillo Negro

447

Morro Colorado

25

La Tablada

619

Montaña Hendida

Tesejerague

Casas
de la Vegueta

4,5

Cortijo
de Diego Alonso

3,5

1

3

Goteras

ya de Terife

Playas Negras

de Ugán

Cortijo
de Chilegua

FV605

Cardón

Cardón

FV618

Corrales
de las Hermosas

593

Tamaretilla

5

Cusa

Montaña Chica

51

Montaña Tirba

5,5

339

FV511

Rosa de los James

Casas de Violante

4

erto Nuevo

402

7,5

FV617

2

Morrete de
Marcos Sanchez

1,5

Carga
del Camello

La Solana

464

FV2

Caracol

FV525

4

195

Rediles

FV56

313

Morro del Majano

323

El Apartadero

Ginigiñam

Playa La Pared

La Pared

5

5

Oasis Park

La Lajita

Tarajalejo

Playa
de Tarajalejo

Punta del
Colorado

Punta
del Caracol

Punta
de Giniginama

Punte
del Pu

FV605

1

Matas Blancas

3

Playa de
la Jaqueta

Punta Paloma

Playa la Lajita

Punta
Cula de la Botija

Punta de los Molinillos

6

Playa de
Matas Blancas

O C É A

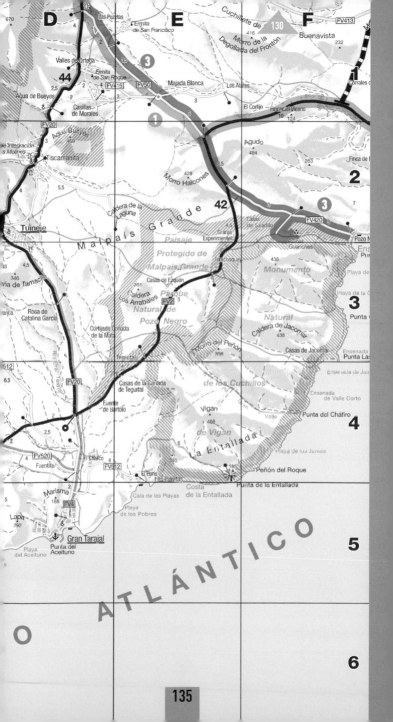

KEY TO ROAD ATLAS

German	Symbol	English
Autobahn · Gebührenpflichtige Anschlussstelle · Gebührenstelle · Anschlussstelle mit Nummer · Rasthaus mit Übernachtung · Raststätte · Kleinraststätte · Tankstelle · Parkplatz mit und ohne WC	Trento	Motorway · Toll junction · Toll station · Junction with number · Motel · Restaurant · Snackbar · Filling-station · Parking place with and without WC
Autobahn in Bau und geplant mit Datum der voraussichtlichen Verkehrsübergabe	Datum Date	Motorway under construction and projected with expected date of opening
Zweibahnige Straße (4-spurig)		Dual carriageway (4 lanes)
Fernverkehrsstraße · Straßennummern	14 E45	Trunk road · Road numbers
Wichtige Hauptstraße		Important main road
Hauptstraße · Tunnel · Brücke		Main road · Tunnel · Bridge
Nebenstraßen		Minor roads
Fahrweg · Fußweg		Track · Footpath
Wanderweg (Auswahl)		Tourist footpath (selection)
Eisenbahn mit Fernverkehr		Main line railway
Zahnradbahn, Standseilbahn		Rack-railway, funicular
Kabinenschwebebahn · Sessellift		Aerial cableway · Chair-lift
Autofähre · Personenfähre		Car ferry · Passenger ferry
Schifffahrtslinie		Shipping route
Naturschutzgebiet · Sperrgebiet		Nature reserve · Prohibited area
Nationalpark · Naturpark · Wald		National park · natural park · Forest
Straße für Kfz. gesperrt	X X X X X	Road closed to motor vehicles
Straße mit Gebühr		Toll road
Straße mit Wintersperre	XII-II	Road closed in winter
Straße für Wohnanhänger gesperrt bzw. nicht empfehlenswert		Road closed or not recommended for caravans
Touristenstraße · Pass	Weinstraße 1510	Tourist route · Pass
Schöner Ausblick · Rundblick · Landschaftlich bes. schöne Strecke		Scenic view · Panoramic view · Route with beautiful scenery
Heilbad · Schwimmbad		Spa · Swimming pool
Jugendherberge · Campingplatz	X X	Youth hostel · Camping site
Golfplatz · Sprungschanze		Golf-course · Ski jump
Kirche im Ort, freistehend · Kapelle		Church · Chapel
Kloster · Klosterruine		Monastery · Monastery ruin
Synagoge · Moschee		Synagogue · Mosque
Schloss, Burg · Schloss-, Burgruine		Palace, castle · Ruin
Turm · Funk-, Fernsehturm		Tower · Radio-, TV-tower
Leuchtturm · Kraftwerk		Lighthouse · Power station
Wasserfall · Schleuse		Waterfall · Lock
Bauwerk · Marktplatz, Areal		Important building · Market place, area
Ausgrabungs- u. Ruinenstätte · Bergwerk		Arch. excavation, ruins · Mine
Dolmen · Menhir · Nuraghen		Dolmen · Menhir · Nuraghe
Hünen-, Hügelgrab · Soldatenfriedhof		Cairn · Military cemetery
Hotel, Gasthaus, Berghütte · Höhle		Hotel, inn, refuge · Cave

Kultur
Malerisches Ortsbild · Ortshöhe — **WIEN** (171) — **Culture**
Picturesque town · Elevation

Eine Reise wert — ★★ **MILANO** — Worth a journey

Lohnt einen Umweg — ★ **TEMPLIN** — Worth a detour

Sehenswert — **Andermatt** — Worth seeing

Landschaft
Eine Reise wert — ★★ **Las Cañadas** — **Landscape**
Worth a journey

Lohnt einen Umweg — ★ **Texel** — Worth a detour

Sehenswert — *Dikti* — Worth seeing

MARCO POLO Erlebnistour 1 — **MARCO POLO Discovery Tour 1**

MARCO POLO Erlebnistouren — **MARCO POLO Discovery Tours**

MARCO POLO Highlight — ⭐ **MARCO POLO Highlight**

MARCO POLO TRAVEL GUIDES

The travel guides with
Insider Tips

INDEX

This index lists all places, sights, and destinations, plus key words and names featured in this guide. Numbers in bold indicate a main entry.

WRITE TO US

e-mail: info@marcopologuides.co.uk

Did you have a great holiday?
Is there something on your mind?
Whatever it is, let us know!
Whether you want to praise, alert us
to errors or give us a personal tip –
MARCO POLO would be pleased to
hear from you.
We do everything we can to provide the
very latest information for your trip.

Nevertheless, despite all of our authors'
thorough research, errors can creep in.
MARCO POLO does not accept any
liability for this. Please contact us by
e-mail or post.

MARCO POLO Travel Publishing Ltd
Pinewood, Chineham Business Park
Crockford Lane, Chineham
Basingstoke, Hampshire RG24 8AL
United Kingdom

PICTURE CREDITS

Cover photograph: Montaña de Escanfraga near Villaverde (Getty Images: R. Eastham & M. Paoli)
Photographs: Casa de la Burra: Marta Cabrera Hernández (19 top; Corbis/JAI: S. Lubenow (96), DuMont Bildarchiv: S. Lubenow (46), Lumma (101, 112 top), Widmann (flap left, 14, 110/111), Zaglitsch (20/21, 29, 49, 64); flonline: Pritz (70/71); f1online/AGE: Melba (18 top); Getty Images: R. Eastham & M. Paoli (1), H. Sorensen (2); Getty Images/Cultura (106/107), Getty Images/Westend61 (3); huber-images: P. Canali (34), M. Rellini (4 top, 32/33, 89, 99), Ripani (59), R. Schmid (4 bottom, 26/27, 37, 41, 54/55, 77, 81, 82, 112 bottom); Laif: Eid (74), Hilger (67), I. Kuerschner (78/79); Look: Frei (60), A. T. Friedel (90/91), Limberger (86), S. Lubenow (7), J. Richter (9, 10, 44, 50, 110); Look/age fotostock (12/13, 17, 31, 113); mauritius images/age (8, 22, 28 left); mauritius images/age fotostock: G. López (19 bottom); mauritius images/AID images/Alamy (43); mauritius images/Alamy (56); mauritius images/Cultura (5, 102/103); mauritius images/CW Images/Alamy (65); mauritius images/foodcollection (18 bottom); mauritius images/iconotec (25); mauritius images/imagebroker: Eisele-Hein (11), Siepmann (28 right, 30/31), Tack (38); mauritius images/imagebroker/68images (6); mauritius images/Science Photos Library (30); picture alliance: R. Hacken (68); picture alliance/Arco Images (105); D. Renckhoff (108, 109, 111), Schapowalow: R. Schmid (63); Schapowalow/SIME: P. Canali (flap right, 72); Skeleton Sea (18 centre); vario images/imagebroker (53, 84/85); vario images/RHPL (124/125)

3rd Edition – fully revised and updated 2019

Worldwide Distribution: Marco Polo Travel Publishing Ltd, Pinewood, Chineham Business Park,
Crockford Lane, Basingstoke, Hampshire RG24 8AL, United Kingdom. Email: sales@marcopolouk.com
© MAIRDUMONT GmbH & Co. KG, Ostfildern
Chief editor: Marion Zorn; Author: Hans-Wilm Schütte; editor: Jochen Schürmann; programme supervision: Lucas Forst-Gill, Susanne Heimburger, Johanna Jiranek, Nikolai Michaelis, Kristin Wittemann, Tim Wohlbold; picture editors: Gabriele Forst, Veronika Plajer
What's hot: wunder media, Munich; Cartography road atlas & pull-out map: © MAIRDUMONT, Ostfildern
Design front cover, p. 1, pull-out map cover: Karl Anders – Büro für Visual Stories, Hamburg; interior: milchhof:atelier, Berlin; Discovery Tours, p. 2/3: Susan Chaaban Dipl.-Des. (FH)
Translated from German by Wendy Barrow, Susan Jones; Prepress: writehouse, Cologne; InterMedia, Ratingen
Phrase book in cooperation with Ernst Klett Sprachen GmbH, Stuttgart, Editorial by Pons Wörterbücher

MIX
Paper from
responsible sources
FSC® C124385
www.fsc.org

DOS & DON'TS ✊

Save yourself some trouble by taking note of the following

DO AVOID SWIMMING ON THE WEST COAST

Except for a few bays that are protected by reefs, the current along the west coast can be very strong and dangerous, especially if you lose your footing. Hardly a year goes by without someone being reckless and drowning.

DO AVOID THE TEMPTATION TO DRIVE CROSS-COUNTRY

Of course it is tempting to take your vehicle off-road but you should definitely not do so in any of the nature parks like the Jandía peninsula or in the dunes of Corralejo. It is a crime and if caught you will liable for a hefty fine.

DON'T RISK GETTING SUNBURNT

Or even heat stroke which can be very serious! A long walk on the first day of your summer holiday (even when it is overcast) could give you a nasty sunburn. This also applies to other times of the year when cool winds can make you forget just how powerful the sun's rays are. Always wear sun screen with a high protection factor – even when it is overcast – and stay out of the sun at midday. Small children and people with sensitive skin are most at risk.

DON'T RISK CATCHING A COLD

Don't be tricked into thinking that Fuerteventura stays warm all year round because of its southern hemisphere location. In winter and early spring, the island is covered by a blanket of clouds and temperatures during the day do not rise above 20 degrees and drop to 15 degrees in the evenings with a strong wind. Make sure to pack a warm jumper, long trousers, windcheater and warm socks.

DON'T BUY CAMERAS, ELECTRONIC GOODS OR WATCHES

There have been numerous reports of customers being cheated so you should exercise extreme caution. You should first check what the goods would cost at home and then also make sure that all the accessories are included. The safest approach to this issue is to simply avoid these items.

DON'T OPT FOR AN ALL INCLUSIVE PACKAGE

Whoever books "all-inclusive" accommodation has to be prepared to pay the prices set by the tour operator. This is usually not a problem in expensive club resorts but can ruin your holiday if you book with low-budget operators. The question to be asked: is self-catering that much more expensive if you only pay for what you really want?